Dossiers

ICC Institute of World Business law

Arbitration and oral evidence

Co-Written by

David Brown
Antonias Dimolitsa
Paul-A. Gélinas
Hans van Houtte
Richard H. Kreindler
Serge Lazareff
Robert S. Rifkind
Anne Véronique Schlaepfer
V.V. Veeder

Co-Edited by

Laurent Lévy and V.V. Veeder

INTERNATIONAL CHAMBER OF COMMERCE
The world business organization

Published in January 2005 by

ICC PUBLISHING S.A.
An affiliate of ICC: the world business organization
38, Cours Albert 1er
75008 Paris – France
www.iccbooks.com

ICC Publication 689
ISBN 92 842 1344 4

Contents

Foreword

By Serge Lazareff
Avocat, France
Chairman, ICC Institute of World Business Law

THE TRADITION IS REBORN!

Arbitration – Money Laundering, Corruption and Fraud, the publication of our 2002 General Annual Meeting, has been a success and the Institute owes its gratitude to its contributors and to ICC Publishing.

The present publication – our General Annual Meeting of 2003 – includes contributions by well-known and respected practitioners on the key issue of "Arbitration and Oral Evidence".

All practitioners of international commercial arbitration have witnessed the considerable progress made over the past years to bring in line different traditions. Roughly speaking, there are no longer major differences between substantive laws or rules of law in the field of international commercial arbitration. Evidence is the only area where there are still different approaches because of legal tradition. The aim of this publication is to give the reader a thorough picture of the practical issues raised by the oral presentation of evidence. Where is the solution? The reader will find in this book the best possible approaches to this key question.

The Institute is endeavouring to discuss at its yearly General Meeting matters of current interest to the arbitration world.

The topic for our AGM 2004 to be held in Paris on 16 November 2004 is "*Parallel State and Arbitral Procedures in International Arbitration*". We have chosen this topic because, as you know, arbitration is suffering today from an excess of procedural questions being raised as preliminary issues. The multiplication of recourses to courts, even when there is a valid arbitration provision, has increased problems raised by parallel proceedings before State and arbitral tribunals. Similarly, Counsel do not hesitate to initiate multiple procedures for the same dispute, even in different countries. Hence, the importance of this topic. Of course, the proceedings of the 2004 AGM will be published.

I thank the reader for his renewed attention to our publications. The Institute hopes to welcome each of you to one of its next events.

With my best regards,

Serge Lazareff
Chairman

Introduction

By V.V. Veeder
Co-Editor
Barrister, Essex Court Chambers, United Kingdom
Council Member, ICC Institute of World Business Law

At the oral hearing, under the adversarial process, the task of the international tribunal deciding factual and expert issues has rarely been more difficult. Yet the original purpose of written witness statements and expert reports was intended to facilitate that task. Arbitrators could work from paper beforehand more easily than oral evidence alone at the main hearing; written witness statements and reports could prepare the parties' counsel more effectively for the hearing than subsequent oral evidence alone; witness statements and expert reports exchanged before that hearing helped prevent "trial by ambush" where, not invariably under the entirely oral procedure, testimony was sprung unheralded at the hearing deliberately to surprise an adverse party (like the white rabbit from the magician's hat); and it was also easier for the less controversial, geographically distant or busy witness: the written statement or report could stand as that witness' evidence-in-chief, subject to oral cross-examination only if required. For all these reasons, oral testimony at the main hearing could be fairer, more efficient and less unpredictable. For arbitration users everywhere, hearing time can be expensive; and uncertainty can preclude effective and timely settlement negotiations.

After two decades of this new practice for transnational arbitration, borrowed from different legal traditions but approximating exactly to none, where then do we stand now? On one view, at the brink of the abyss. Written witness statements can bear little relation to the independent recollection of the factual witness, with draft after draft being crafted by the party's lawyer or the party itself, with the witness's written evidence becoming nothing more than special pleading, usually expressed at considerable length. It rarely contains the actual, unassisted recollection of the witness expressed in his or her own actual words. Accordingly, in the eyes of certain arbitrators, the use (or abuse) of witness statements has made them unreliable, expensive and often unfair. Still worse, with the cloak of legal professional privilege (together with the continued absence of any global code of ethics for arbitration practitioners), witness statements can be subjected to unsavoury practices. And expert reports, albeit relatively a smaller problem, can result from ill-informed or over-imaginative expertise as to the relevant facts; or even the work of technical advocates, rather than independent experts seeking objectively to assist the arbitration tribunal. Justice, truth, fairness and efficiency are thus all ill served; and the pure well of oral testimony at the main hearing has become gravely polluted by the current practice of written witness statements and expert reports.

On another view, a superlative procedure has evolved unique to international arbitration, neither common law nor civilian, neither anglo-saxon nor francophone, neither English nor US, neither fish nor fowl. The written exposition of expert opinions allows experts to agree expert issues or to agree on the reasons why they disagree long before the main hearing, thereby facilitating the task of the parties' counsel and arbitrators but also greatly enhancing the possibility of an amicable settlement before the main hearing; the written witness statement allows much of the factual brushwood to be cleared from the arbitral stage, leaving only the critically important issues to be addressed orally at the main hearing; and only forensic dinosaurs could desire a return to the old "trial by ambush", including the dramatic production of white rabbits. Indeed, the new procedure (albeit now not so new) has grown so superlative that it is no longer unique: it is copied by national State courts for their reforms to civil procedure, such as England (in the Commercial Court and, more widely, with Lord Woolf's recent reforms). Accordingly, albeit discarding deliberate abuse which can infiltrate any procedure, the mixed written and oral procedure serves well efficiency, fairness, truth and justice at the main hearing.

The following papers from distinguished practitioners and arbitrators demonstrate with succinct clarity that the true position lies somewhere between these different views. There is grave disquiet at certain of the more alarming practices (or potential practices) developing with witness statements, particularly in the absence of an appropriate opportunity for effective cross-examination by the adverse party's counsel; but there is no pressing demand for an arbitral retreat into the primeval slime. It seems generally accepted that an overall benefit will result from developing what is generally good and redressing what is only partly wrong – without spoiling the whole. There is perhaps a need to understand better what is good and what is wrong on the part of both practitioners and arbitrators; and a balance must be struck (or re-struck) between efficiency and fairness, without injustice. How far was the subject of much debate at this seminar. As these papers make clear, there is no single, easy answer. International arbitration is not a pure science; and international arbitrators do not practise their craft as if painting by numbers. Of all developments, the most important may now be transparency: if the witness has been assisted by others in producing his or her witness written statement, then the witness should be required to disclose in the statement their names and professions, the time taken and the form of assistance provided by them; and as regards experts, the report should also record the expert's understanding of his independent and overriding duty to assist the arbitration tribunal as an expert, not an advocate. These and other good general practices can only encourage both fairness and efficiency in the receipt of oral testimony at the main hearing.

1

Giving evidence:

Some reflections on oral evidence vs documentary evidence and on the obligations and rights of the witnesses

By Antonias Dimolitsa
Partner, A. Dimolitsa & Associates, Greece
Council Member, ICC Institute of World Business Law

INTRODUCTION

It seems advisable to recall some key factors which are to be taken into account during all the discussions we may have on the subject of the present Annual Meeting of the Institute:

- One of the reasons why parties to an international contract decide to have recourse to arbitration is to avoid the uncertainties and problems inherent in national court proceedings.
- The organisation of the proceedings is left to the autonomy of the parties and the arbitrators, who are not under any obligation to apply the rules of procedure of a national law (Art. 15(1) ICC Rules of Arbitration, Art. 14(1) and (2) LCIA Arbitration Rules, Art. 16(1) AAA International Arbitration Rules, Art. 15(1) UNCITRAL Arbitration Rules, Art. 19 UNCITRAL Model Law, Art. 1494 French NCPC, Art. 182(1) and (2) of the Swiss PIL Statute). We are in front of the phenomenon of *"délégalisation"*[1] of arbitration proceedings.
- Experience has shown that there is no categorical divide between civil law and common law in international arbitration[2], and that a specific procedural system has developed which contains distilled influences from both systems.
- The "IBA Rules on the Taking of Evidence in International Commercial Arbitration (1999)" are the result of the actual rapprochement of the two systems as regards taking of evidence in international arbitration. The

parties and the arbitrators may adopt all or part of the IBA Rules, or use them as guidelines or as a source of inspiration when freely determining the procedural rules of their own arbitration.

- It is the arbitral tribunal's duty to ensure that evidence is taken in an efficient and economical manner, while also ensuring "equality of arms" between parties from different legal traditions. The procedural rules governing the taking of evidence must be determined in advance in each case, to avoid surprising the parties and their counsel during the proceedings.

ORAL EVIDENCE VS DOCUMENTARY EVIDENCE

1. Impact of the composition of the arbitral tribunal

It is true that the legal culture of an arbitrator may influence the way the arbitrator will determine the rules on the taking of evidence, admit or not certain persons as witnesses, conduct their hearing, intervene during their examination and, most importantly, assess the evidence submitted by weighing differently the documentary and the oral evidence. Some fourteen years ago Professor Claude Reymond stated during an Annual Meeting on a similar subject: *"However we must have no illusions: nobody approaches a procedure* [...] *with a mind totally freed of his usual way of thinking and of his conception of the requirements of justice"*[3].

This may well be always true from a psychological viewpoint. However, in practice, experienced arbitrators are capable of adopting different approaches in order to respond to the wishes of the parties and their counsel in homogeneous arbitration proceedings and, in "transnational" proceedings, of making use of the best of both systems (civil law/common law), and defining suitable rules. In the latter arbitration proceedings, which are the most usual ones, equilibrium is attained between oral and documentary evidence and there are not really big divergences in the rules that are finally applied, though the arbitrators come from differing legal traditions. Moreover, in most cases, the arbitral tribunal, in light of the arguments put forward by the parties' counsel and of the particular facts of the case, succeeds in finding its internal cultural equilibrium in the way it will approach and assess the evidence.

Needless to revert to the importance of the choice of the arbitrators (especially, but not only, of the chairman). An ineffable quality in the international arbitrator is however reminded and stressed in the present context: the open-mindedness, which presupposes but does not coincide with neutrality.

2. Respective values and roles

■ Documentary evidence

"Documentary evidence is the most precise and reliable means of evidence: a fact established in a document can – as a general rule – be held as a certainty, subject only to forgery"[4].

Documentary evidence has a preponderant role in international arbitration, and this seems normal in the context of international business. Indeed, in most cases, the parties have signed a written agreement and have exchanged correspondence and other documents which they have kept on file. The parties use these documents to support or prove the legal grounds or points of fact they are submitting. Moreover, according to a general practice, these documents are enclosed with the parties' first submissions. An initial establishment of the facts of the case based on documents can therefore be completed fairly quickly, before any hearing.

The production of documents[5], which is very common in practice, supplements – irrespective of whether the documents are produced voluntarily or following an order by the arbitral tribunal – the documentary evidence. As a consequence, witnesses are thus at times relegated to a secondary role. However, in some cases precisely because of the sheer volume of the documentation, with the parties submitting thousands of documents, the arbitral tribunal, in its attempt to identify the key points in the huge case file, will turn to witnesses demanding precise details and clarifications; witnesses may thus regain their essential role.

It is difficult to measure the influence that the civil law tradition has exerted on the role of documentary evidence in international arbitration proceedings. One should rather perceive this role as a direct result of arbitration's omnipresent pragmatism.

■ Oral evidence[6]

The testimony *"is the eldest evidence, the most indispensable and widespread. Once two people are confronted in a dispute, there is need to call in witnesses of fact in order to decide who is right"*[7].

Nowadays, regarding international arbitration, one may say, first, that the testimonies of witnesses supplement documentary evidence when the latter is insufficient. Second, that there is often a real need for witnesses to provide additional information or clarify certain points. Moreover, quite apart from any theoretical discussion on the inquisitorial or "accusatory" (in the French meaning of "accusatoire") role of the judge/arbitrator, the generally used method for conducting evidentiary hearings, which is largely based on the common law system, contributes to achieving the above objectives. Oral evidence also satisfies such other need of the arbitral tribunal, which is linked to the very nature of arbitration, that is to meet the people involved in the performance of the contractual relationship in order to gain a better understanding, do better in general, and progress more effectively towards forming its conviction.

The taking of oral evidence, as a second phase of the establishment of the facts of the case, is in practice regarded as *a priori* necessary in order to find the "truth" which the arbitral tribunal will lay down in the reasoning of the award. What is meant is, of course, only a relative truth[8], the truth which the arbitral tribunal will retain, after having freely weighed and assessed all the evidence submitted (documentary and oral).

■ Suitability of oral or documentary evidence in a given case

As a rule, both types of evidence – documentary and oral – are used in most international arbitration cases, in compliance with the applicable institutional rules and with what was agreed by the arbitrators and the parties at the start of the proceedings and subsequently confirmed and specified in procedural orders. This combined evidentiary procedure corresponds, in principle, to the real will of the parties and the arbitrators, notwithstanding the fact that at times, for practical reasons related to the insufficiency of one type of evidence, the other type of evidence may acquire more weight.

It may however happen, during a particular arbitration case, that the question arises for discussion between the arbitrators and the parties as to whether an evidentiary hearing is actually necessary. It is generally accepted that the arbitral tribunal may rule solely on the basis of documentary evidence if the parties so request or agree to this; that is in the latter case, if the tribunal considers that the documentary evidence is sufficient and permits the establishment of the facts of the case and their assessment and if the parties consent to the non-examination of witnesses (Art. 20(6) ICC Rules of Arbitration, Art. 19(1) LCIA Arbitration Rules, Art. 15(2) UNCITRAL Arbitration Rules, Art. 24(1) UNCITRAL Model Law).

The entire question "which type of evidence should be chosen – documentary or oral?" can only be raised internally between a party and its counsel, when preparing the evidence they will submit in support of their case. Arguably, the answer depends to a great extent on the legal culture of the party and its counsel. So one may be inclined to believe that lawyers from common law countries who are used to the pre-trial procedure will quite comfortably produce all documents they have in their possession, even when these undermine their position, while paying particular attention to the preparation and *mise en scène* of the hearing of witnesses. In contrast, lawyers from civil law countries will have a tendency to closely examine all the documents in their possession and, if they consider that these are not pertinent, or not sufficiently favourable to their case, or even dangerous, they will probably hold them back and focus, without great enthusiasm, on the preparation of the witnesses available (risking even an order on production of documents); if, on the contrary, they consider that their client's case can be argued on the basis of the documentary evidence alone, they may decide to forgo oral evidence.

The above are rather theoretical, however, as the persons engaged by the parties as counsel more often than not have considerable experience in international arbitration, and are at times even "too professional". Instead of relying on preconceived national procedural approaches, they implement carefully considered strategies developed in view of the strong and weak points of the case, and make full use of the flexibility of arbitration proceedings.

Be that as it may, the arbitral tribunal has absolute control over the taking of evidence. It can, accordingly, refuse further evidence – be it the production of a document or the hearing of a witness – if it considers that the facts have already been sufficiently established or that the evidence offered is not relevant and material. Conversely, it can summon a party to produce additional evidence of any kind, at any time (Art. 20(5) ICC Rules of Arbitration, Art. 24(3) UNCITRAL Arbitration Rules, Art. 8(4) IBA Rules).

OBLIGATIONS AND RIGHTS OF THE WITNESSES

1. Obligation to appear, to take the oath, to testify, to tell the truth

There is need to differentiate between parties and third-parties. There is also need to differentiate between appearing and testifying, on the one hand, and telling the truth, on the other.

■ Appearing and testifying

As regards the parties (and their representatives), it could be assumed that they have an obligation if summoned by the arbitral tribunal, but also a right if they so wish, to appear and testify. This obligation[9] and right vis-à-vis the arbitral tribunal would derive from the arbitration agreement and from the arbitral "process ties" (*"liens d'instance"*) marked by the private character of arbitration and the element of trust[10]. It is further suggested that the parties' obligation to act fairly in the contractual relationship is extended into the dispute. The obligation to inform, being a specific application of the good faith principle[11], could be operative even during the arbitration proceedings. Thus, each party would have an obligation vis-à-vis the other party to appear as witnesses if so requested by the latter, and to explain why the contractual relationship has deteriorated into a dispute.

Having said that, the question arises whether an arbitrator has the power to summon a party to appear as witness on *astreinte*[12]. The answer should be in the affirmative, if one accepts that the obligation for a party to appear as a witness does actually exist and if he shares the opinion that the *astreinte* is a private sanction and not a means of enforcement, in other words a juridical police measure within the sphere of arbitral jurisdiction[13].

As for third-parties, one might advance that legislation such as Article 10(1) of the French Civil Code[14], or other similar provisions in other countries, could be transposed and applied to international arbitration. We should not delude ourselves, however. This type of provision, which imposes a civic obligation on any person to cooperate with the judicial authorities so that truth be revealed, only concerns the interest of the public service of the national judicial system, and is tied to the judge's *imperium*, which is essential in order to compel someone to cooperate. In international arbitration, any "obligation" incumbent upon a third-party, which by definition is extraneous to the arbitral proceedings, to appear and testify cannot but be based on a specific legal relationship binding said third-party to one of the parties in the arbitration proceedings. In the absence of any such relationship, there would be no obligation; the third-party would be voluntarily rendering a service on the request of one of the parties, whether or not motivated by an underlying interest.

■ Telling the truth

Is it possible to differentiate between testifying and telling the truth[15]? It depends on what truth we are talking about. Such a differentiation is not inconceivable if we accept that a testimony does not necessarily disclose everything the witness[16] has seen, heard or known. In other words, a differentiation might be conceivable, if we accept that it is possible to give an honest testimony that does not contain the "whole truth".

Yet, who draws the line between testifying and telling the truth, and how? Arguably, it is the counsel representing the party which calls the witness, and the witness himself, when preparing the witness's written statement and/or his appearance before the arbitral tribunal. This means it is the cultural back-ground and integrity of the counsel and the witness that will dictate the substance of the testimony, which is nevertheless given with the objective of serving the interests of one of the parties and is based on a desire to win that party's case. The above stand irrespective of the quality of a witness as representative or employee of a party, or as third-party. We are here before a real challenge to look for the golden rule between pragmatism and honesty. We should not forget, however, that as a result of the cross-examination any testimony – even those prepared with all due professional integrity – may be reformed and let emerge or permit the approach to the "whole truth".

In any event, there is a valid deontological obligation incumbent upon the counsel[17] – confirmed as far as European counsel is concerned by the CCBE[18] – and a moral obligation incumbent upon the witness to, at the least, refrain from knowingly giving false or misleading information to the arbitral tribunal.

■ Taking the oath

The device of taking the oath in itself introduces an obligation to tell the truth. And, precisely, the very danger of this device is that the witness is expected to have complied with such obligation[19]. Certainly, it is not because international arbitrators do not care about the truth that in practice they do not require witnesses to take the oath, and prefer to ask them to simply state, without any formality, that they will tell the truth[20]. In general, arbitrators, as private individuals, do not feel qualified to administer the oath. This is also the position adopted in the national laws of several countries, including Germany, France, Sweden, Italy and Greece. However, the UK (Sect. 38(5) of the Arbitration Act 1996), Belgium (Art. 1696(3) of the Belgian Judicial Code

(CJB)) and the Netherlands (Art. 1041(1) of the Netherlands Code of Civil Procedure (WBR)) expressly confer this power on arbitrators. In Switzerland, there seems to be some debate over this issue.

In any event, when witnesses give oral evidence they are required by the arbitral tribunal to tell the truth and are at the same time informed of the possible consequences of false testimony under the law of the place of arbitration. As regards taking the oath before the arbitrators, or before a national judge within the context of court assistance, this would matter only if it was a condition of penalising false testimony (Germany, UK, France, Italy) or a cause for a harsher sentence (see, for example, Articles 224-225 of the Greek Penal Code and, in particular, Art. 307 of the Swiss Penal Code).

It could thus be argued that although a witness has an obligation to tell the truth, he does not have an obligation to take the oath in international arbitration proceedings; on the contrary, he has a right to refuse to take the oath without necessarily having to justify his refusal on religious grounds. Taking the oath does not fit the private, multicultural, autonomous and secular nature of arbitration.

2. Sanctions in case of non-compliance with duties of a witness

■ Refusal to appear and testify

The arbitral tribunal may order at any time the appearance of a witness identified by the parties, but also order any party to provide the appearance of any other person to testify (Art. 20(5) ICC Rules of Arbitration, Art. 4(11) IBA Rules). If a witness who has submitted a witness statement does not appear to an evidentiary hearing without valid reason, the arbitral tribunal may decide to disregard his written statement or infer that such evidence would be adverse to the interests of the party that offered the witness. If, on the other hand, a party is ordered to provide the appearance of a person as a witness and such person refuses to appear, it is difficult to see any consequences, unless the witness is a party or a party's representative.

Arbitrators cannot compel a person to appear and testify. However, if they consider it extremely important to hear a person who has refused to appear, they can apply to a national court[21] (as a case of generally accepted court assistance – more expressly provided under Art. 184(2), of the Swiss PIL Statute and Sect. 43 of the Arbitration Act 1996), and even use the procedure of international rogatory letters[22].

The question of sanctions for refusal to appear and testify can only arise when an arbitral tribunal has asked a national court to compel a witness to appear. In such a case, the sanctions will obviously depend on the common procedural law in the country of the court; they will most often take the form of a fine.

■ False testimony

We need to differentiate between sanctions *stricto sensu* under common criminal law, which are applied against the witness himself, and sanctions *lato sensu* or rather "arbitral" remedies for the effects of false testimony.

The sanctions *stricto sensu* for false testimony are sanctions of criminal law. With the exception of Swiss law, the national provisions of criminal law on false testimony – whether or not an oath was taken – are based on the notion of public service of the national judicial system and do not refer to arbitration. In consideration of the private nature of arbitration, and the autonomy which characterises the arbitration proceedings, one might say that their application by analogy is by no means evident and even add that such an application does not seem advisable: to moralise arbitration, yes, but not through its judiciarization. In any event, it would be easier to conceive the application by analogy of such sanctions, if the testimony was given with the assistance of a court.

Swiss law expressly provides (Art. 309 of the Swiss Penal Code) that the provisions concerning false representations by a party (Art. 306) or false testimony by a third-party (Art. 307) apply also to arbitration proceedings. However, this provision has been criticised by some authors[23], who consider that there is not a sufficiently precise legal basis for indictment of a witness for false testimony or, even more so, against a party for false representations, because the evidentiary process in arbitration is not set in law but is left, to a large extent, to the discretion of the parties. Yet, this unique and actually very harsh[24] provision does not seem to be applied in practice.

Generally speaking, criminal proceedings initiated exclusively for false testimony before an arbitral tribunal, if they exist, must be very rare and there are no examples of any published case law. We can only stop at some questions which may arise and need to be clarified if an action for false testimony is to be brought before a national court:

- The actual possibility of initiating criminal proceedings before the national courts of a given country (would this be the country of nationality of the witness or of the place of arbitration?); applicability of national criminal law to international arbitration; immunity of the witness (USA); only sworn false testimony is punishable (Germany, UK, France);
- Applicable law: normally this would be the law of the place of arbitration as *lex loci delicti commissi* and not the law that applies to the merits of the dispute;
- The necessary elements to establish the crime or offence of false testimony in accordance with the applicable law: is the witness's deliberate distortion of the truth sufficient, or must it be established that the untruthful statements have influenced – or could have influenced – the outcome of arbitration and caused – or could have caused – prejudice? Should the untruthful statements have been made with malicious intent?
- The accused witness's personal lines of defence (such as, he could not have told the truth without seriously and unavoidably jeopardising his freedom or integrity);
- The possibility of filing a criminal complaint accompanied by a civil suit for damages on the basis of other criminal provisions, if the elements establishing other offences or crimes actually exist, such as – and in particular – fraud, deceit, defamation. The clarification of this point is important, because the real interest and objective of the injured party initiating criminal proceedings will normally be to obtain recovery and not to see a witness fined or given a prison sentence.

The answers to all these questions will depend on the applicable criminal law and the solutions in comparative law vary[25].

As regards sanctions *lato sensu* or rather "arbitral" remedies for the effects of false testimony, first and foremost we should not forget that any false testimony may be disregarded by the arbitral tribunal and may even have the opposite to the desired consequences in the award, that is against the party it aimed to favour. This implies, of course, that the untruth is discovered during the arbitration proceedings. In practice, this often happens as a result of effective cross-examination and/or following thorough study of the file and, in particular, following the comparison of oral evidence with documentary evidence by the arbitrators. Needless to say, the arbitrators' qualities, among which their vigilance, will play a very important role.

However, we cannot exclude the possibility that a false testimony may, on the contrary, have served as the basis for an award. In this type of situation, it is the award that will be prejudicial to one of the parties and said party will seek "remedy" for the award.

We know that as a general rule the court which sets aside or enforces an arbitral award does not scrutinise the reasons on which the tribunal based its decision. Accordingly, an award based on false testimony is not, in principle, subject to any remedy. However, in exceptional and extreme cases where false testimony constitutes fraud, the award ceases to be immune. Comparative law has identified four solutions[26] to this type of problem: the award is set aside on the grounds that it is contrary to public policy[27], the award is reconsidered by the judicial authority[28], the award is reconsidered by the arbitrators[29], the award is reconsidered by the arbitrators if leave is given to this effect by the judicial authority[30].

The few existing examples show that for the award to be set aside or reconsidered new and material facts, which the applicant was not in the position to invoke previously, must establish that there was a genuine procedural fraud on which the award was based[31]. It is only in such cases that the national court, and/or the arbitral tribunal if it is still constituted or can meet again, will preclude in one way or another the "unfair" effects of the award. It is finally noted that the advisability *de lege ferenda* of a special procedure for the revision of international arbitration awards is a present-day issue at least in France[32].

END NOTES

1 Berthold Goldman, "Instance judiciaire et instance arbitrale internationale" in Etudes offertes à Pierre Bellet, Litec 1991, p. 219 et seq.

2 If there is such a divide it would rather refer to the United States legal system; because with respect to Great Britain, Canada, Australia and New Zealand, one may seriously wonder whether their systems are closer to the "European civil law" or the "US common law".

3 "*Mais il ne faut pas se faire d'illusion: nul n'aborde une procédure,* [...], *avec un esprit entièrement libéré de ses habitudes de pensée et de sa conception des exigences de la justice*", "Taking of evidence in international arbitral proceedings", in The Dossiers of the Institute of International Business Law and Practice, No. 8/1989, ICC Publishing No. 440/8 1990, Conclusions, p. 165 et seq.

4 "*La preuve écrite est le moyen de preuve le plus précis et celui dont l'authenticité est la moins sujette à caution: un fait constaté dans un titre peut – en règle générale – être considéré comme certain, sous la réserve de la fausseté du titre*", Walter J. Habscheid, Droit Judiciaire Privé Suisse, second edition, Librairie de l'Université Georg et Cie S.A., Geneva 1981, p. 446.

5 Or *discovery*, which has a limited meaning in international arbitration, namely the production of documents that are limited, identifiable, relevant and material to the outcome of the case (see Art. 3 – IBA Rules of Evidence).

6 Here, we will use the term oral evidence to cover testimonies of any kind, including testimonies by the parties' representatives and their employees, with the sole exception of testimonies by expert-witnesses, who form a separate category of witness.

7 [Le témoignage] "*est la plus ancienne des preuves, la plus nécessaire et la plus répandue. Dès que deux hommes se sont affrontés dans un litige, on a dû faire appel aux témoins du fait pour les départager*", J. Graven in "Droit et vérité", publication of the Faculty of Law of the University of Geneva – 1946, p. 127.

8 "*The 'truth' found in both judicial and arbitral proceedings is relative rather than absolute. It is derived from the evidence presented by the parties and is dependent upon the standard of proof applied to the evidence. Thus, the same evidence could produce one result in a criminal case in a common law country where the standard of proof is 'beyond a reasonable doubt' and a different result in a civil case where the standard is the 'preponderance of the evidence'*". See Robert von Mehren, "The Burden of Proof in International Arbitration" in Planning Efficient Arbitration Proceedings, The Law Applicable

in International Arbitration, ICCA Congress Series No. 7 (1994), p. 123, note 3. Compare with Bruno Oppetit: *"the civil process is based on the discovery of a truth, albeit a relative truth, that the judge must try to get to by adopting an approach based as closely as possible on the realities of the case, as is shown by recent legislation on the manifestation of the truth in legal proceedings",* ["*le procès civil est ordonné à la découverte d'une vérité, relative certes, mais que le juge doit tenter d'atteindre par une approche aussi exacte que possible de la réalité, comme en témoignent les dispositions législatives récentes relatives à la manifestation de la vérité en justice*"], "Les rôles respectifs du juge et du technicien dans l'administration de la preuve en droit privé", PUF 1976, p. 54.

9 On such an obligation under French law see Art. 11(1) NCPC, which also applies to arbitration (Art. 1460(2) NCPC): "*The parties are required to co-operate in view of the establishment of the facts of the case, and the judge will draw his conclusions from any failure or refusal to co-operate*" ["*Les parties sont tenues d'apporter leur concours aux mesures d'instruction sauf au juge à tirer toute conséquence d'une abstention ou d'un refus*"].

10 A distinguished French author has stressed regarding trust in international arbitration: "*A decisive factor in the success of arbitration ... it is because this element is at the very heart of the concept of arbitration and also the basis of business relations, especially international business relations, where international commercial arbitration has taken off so dramatically, to the extent that it now plays a preponderant role in the legal and economic life of societies*" [*"Facteur décisif de la réussite de l'arbitrage... c'est parce que cet élément* [la confiance] *se trouve à la fois au cœur du concept même de l'arbitrage et à la base des relations commerciales, surtout internationales, où l'arbitrage commercial international a pris cet essor irrésistible qui lui confère aujourd'hui un rôle de premier plan dans la vie juridique et économique des peuples"*], Henri Motulsky, "Ecrits, Etudes et notes sur l'arbitrage", Dalloz 1974, p. 510.

11 See Yves Derains, "Les tendances de la jurisprudence arbitrale internationale", J.D.I. 4, 1993, p. 829, especially p. 847 et seq.

12 This concept of civil law means a periodic fine for delay in performance, in the present context for delay in compliance with the summons.

13 See Charles Jarrosson, "Réflexions sur l'imperium" in Etudes Pierre Bellet, p. 245, especially p. 272-273.

14 Art. 10 of the French Civil Code: "*Everyone is bound to cooperate with the courts for the emergence of the truth. Anyone who, without any legitimate reason, evades such an obligation imposed upon him by law, may be compelled to comply, if necessary on astreinte or a civil fine, without prejudice*

to any damages that may be awarded". ["*Chacun est tenu d'apporter son concours à la justice en vue de la manifestation de la vérité. Celui qui, sans motif légitime, se soustrait à cette obligation lorsqu'il en a été légalement requis, peut être contraint d'y satisfaire, au besoin à peine d'astreinte ou d'amende civile, sans préjudice de dommages et intérêts*"].

15 The Greek word for "witness" is **μάρτυς**, that is "martyr"; in modern Greek the same word is used for the witness and the martyr. In ancient Greek, **μάρτυς** signified the person who was declaring/confirming the truth he knew. Influenced by Christianism, **μάρτυς** acquired the additional meaning of the person who declares the truth of the Gospel and is ready to sacrifice himself for it.

16 Meaning all witnesses, parties and third-parties. Because in civil proceedings, according to many national laws, parties are not required to testify on facts that undermine their own interests ("*nemo tenetur edere contra se*", right to silence).

17 See on this question the remarkable article of V.V. Veeder "The 2001 Goff Lecture. The Lawyer's Duty to Arbitrate in Good Faith", in Arbitration International, Vol.18, No. 4, (2002), p. 431.

18 See Art. 4(4) of the Code of Conduct for Lawyers in the European Community (CCBE) which also applies to relations between lawyers and arbitrators (Art. 4(5)).

19 Henri Batiffol, "Observations sur la preuve des faits", in La preuve en droit, Travaux centre de logique de Bruxelles, 1981, p. 308.

20 Just the truth, and not "*the truth, the whole truth and nothing but the truth*" (Art. 35(2) of the ICSID Arbitration Rules). Is there another example of the pragmatism of international arbitration?

21 See the order issued by the arbitral tribunal in the case ICC 6401, 1 October 1990, points 1 and 2, J.D.I. 4, 1998, p. 1067, obs. Dominique Hascher; Order issued by the Geneva First Instance Court (Tribunal de première instance de Genève), 15 October 1990, Bull. ASA 1994, p. 307.

22 See order issued by the arbitral tribunal in case ICC 6401, 1 October 1990, op. cit., supra note 21, point 5; Order issued by the Geneva First Instance Court, 31 January 1991, addressing rogatory letters to the authorities of Vaduz (Liechtenstein) and Paris (France), Bull. ASA 1994, p. 310; Order issued by the Geneva First Instance Court, 16 February 1993 addressing rogatory letters to the competent authorities in Aix-en-Provence (France), Heidelberg (Germany) and Solama Beach (California-USA), Bull. ASA 1994, p. 314; Order issued by the Geneva First Instance Court, 5 January 1993, addressing rogatory letters to the competent authorities in Boston (USA), Bull. ASA 1994, p. 316.

23 See Martin Schubarth – Ursula Cassani, Commentaire du droit pénal suisse, Code pénal suisse – special section, Volume 9: "Crimes ou délits contre l'administration de la justice", Articles 303-311 CP, Staempfli and Cie SA Berne, 1996, p. 139 et seq.

24 The testimony does not need to be significant for the decision. Nor does Art. 307 of the Swiss Penal Code assume that the witness is aware of the significance of his testimony and that he deliberately seeks to influence the decision. The witness must, however, be aware that his testimony is false.

25 See, on the diversity of solutions in comparative law: Marianne Roth, "False Testimony at International Arbitration Hearings Conducted in England and Switzerland, A Comparative View", Journal of International Arbitration, Vol. 11, No. 1, March 1994, p. 5 et seq.; Christoph Liebscher, "The Challenge of Awards on the Basis of Criminal Acts", in ICCA Congress Series No.11, International Commercial Arbitration: Important Contemporary Questions, ICCA International Arbitration Congress London 2002, p. 300 et seq.

26 See Yves Derains, "La révision des sentences dans l'arbitrage international" in Law of International Business and Dispute Settlement in the 21st Century, Liber Amicorum Karl-Heinz Böckstiegel, 2001, p. 165, especially p. 169.

27 UNCITRAL Model Law (preparatory work) and French law, which expressly rules out the possibility of a revision of international arbitration awards (Art. 1507 NCPC); see in particular Paris Court of Appeal, 10 September 1998, SA Thomson CSF vs Société Brunner Sociedade Civil de Administracao Limitada and Société Frontier AG Bern, Rev. arb. 2001, p. 583, obs. Jean-Baptiste Racine. This solution has been criticised by some authors: see Yves Derains, op. cit., supra note 26, and Ibrahim Fadlallah "Nouveau recul de la révision au fond: motivation et fraude dans le contrôle des sentences arbitrales internationales", Gazette du Palais, Les cahiers de l'arbitrage (No. 2), December 2000, p. 5 et seq. See also other national laws with specific mention of fraud as ground for annulment: Art. 595 Austrian Code of Civil Procedure; Art. 857 (8) and 544 (6) Greek Code of Civil Procedure; Art. 801 Japanese Code of Civil Procedure; Sect. 10 (a) of the US FAA.

28 Art. 1068 Netherlands Code of Civil Procedure; Art. 43 of the Spanish law 60/2003 on arbitration of 23 December 2003.

29 Revision of an award by arbitration is explicitly provided in Art. 51 (3) of the ICSID Convention. In case law, see the French Cour de Cassation in Fougerolle vs Procofrance, 25 May 1992, Rev. arb. 1993, p. 91: "*it results from the general principles of law on fraud that, notwithstanding Art. 1507 of the New Code of Civil Procedure which prohibits any application for revision of an award, an international arbitration award made in France may, exceptionally in case of fraud, be retracted if the arbitral tribunal is still constituted after the award has*

been made (or can meet again)" ["il résulte des principes généraux du droit en matière de fraude que, nonobstant l'exclusion du recours en révision par l'art. 1507 NCPC, la rétractation d'une sentence rendue en France en matière d'arbitrage international doit être, exceptionnellement, admise en cas de fraude lorsque le tribunal arbitral demeure constitué après le prononcé de la sentence (ou peut à nouveau être réuni)."]. See also on an application to reconsider a partial award filed directly during the proceedings with the arbitral tribunal sitting in Washington in the *ad hoc* arbitration Antoine Biloune (Syria) and Marine Drive Complex Ltd. (Ghana) vs Ghana Investments Centre and the Government of Ghana, Y. B. Com. Arb. XIX (1994), p. 11 et seq. After noting that Articles 35, 36 and 37 of the UNCITRAL Arbitration Rules do not allow the possibility of challenging awards, the tribunal ruled:

"[33] Nevertheless, a court or Tribunal, including this international arbitral Tribunal, has an inherent power to take cognisance of credible evidence, timely placed before it, that its previous determinations were the product of false testimony, forged documents or other egregious 'fraud on the Tribunal' [...] *Certainly if such corruption or fraud in the evidence would justify an international or a national court in voiding or refusing to enforce the award, this Tribunal also, so long as it still has jurisdiction over the dispute, can take necessary corrective action.* [...] *[34] The present Tribunal would not hesitate to reconsider and modify its earlier award were it shown by credible evidence that it had been the victim of fraud and that its determinations in the previous award were the product of false testimony. However, no such evidence has been adduced ".*

See also for the same views and on the "inherent authority" of the tribunal to reconsider awards in exceptional circumstances, the awards Dames and Moore and Ram Industries of the Iran-United States Claims Tribunal, Charles N. Brower, Jason D. Brueschke "The Iran – United States Claims Tribunal", Martinus Nijhof Publishers 1998, Chapter 7 (Reconsideration and Reopening of Awards), p. 242-260.

30 As is the case in England and Wales, see Sect. 68(2)(g) and (3) of the Arbitration Act 1996; see also on Swiss law, Swiss Tribunal Fédéral, 11 March 1992, Rev. arb. 1993, p. 115 et seq., obs. P.Y. Tschanz, the grounds listed in Art. 137 of the Federal Law on the Organisation of the Judicial System (OJF).

31 See High Court, Queen's Bench Division (Commercial Court), 19 December 1997, Westacre Investments Inc. (Panama) vs (1) Judoimport-SDPR Holdings Co. Ltd. (F.R. Yugo); (2) Beogradska Banka (F.R. Yugo); (3) The Federal Directorate of Supply and Procurement of the Federal Republic of Yugoslavia (F.R. Yugo); (4) Beogradska Banka DD (F.R. Yugo), Y.B. Com. Arb. XXIII (1998), p. 836 et seq., concerning enforcement proceedings of an ICC award rendered in Switzerland during which defendants argued, *inter alia*, that the award was made as a result of false testimony given under oath:

"Where a party to a foreign New York Convention arbitration award alleges at the enforcement stage that it has been obtained by perjured evidence that party will not normally be permitted to adduce in the English courts additional evidence to make good that allegation unless it is established that:

(i) the evidence sought to be adduced is of sufficient cogency and weight to be likely to have materially influenced the arbitrators' conclusion had it been advanced at the hearing; and

(ii) the evidence was not available or reasonably obtainable either

(a) at the time of the hearing of the arbitration; or

(b) at such time as would have enabled the party concerned to have adduced it in the court of supervisory jurisdiction to support an application to reverse the arbitrators' award if such procedure were available".

Precisely, the interested party could have filed an application for revision of the award in Switzerland, but did not do so.

See also for the same views, Swiss Tribunal Fédéral 11 May 1999, Bull. ASA 2000, p. 323 et seq. and the award Ram Industries (on the allegation of forged documents and false testimony), The Iran-United States Claims Tribunal, op.cit, supra note 29.

32 See Yves Derains, op. cit., supra note 26; Ibrahim Fadlallah, op. cit., supra note 27; Dominique Hascher, "La révision en arbitrage international", in Liber Amicorum Claude Reymond, Litec 2004, p. 111.

2

Evidence through witnesses

By Paul-A. Gélinas
Member of the Montreal and Paris Bars
Council Member, ICC Institute of World Business Law

INTRODUCTION

An attractive characteristic of international arbitration lies in its built-in flexibility; each case is unique and experienced arbitrators will tailor the procedural rules to fit the specifics of the dispute at hand, having regards to the cultural environment from which the parties originate and to the legal training of their counsel. The purpose of this chapter is to examine how the freedom enjoyed by the parties and the arbitrators in organizing the conduct of evidentiary hearings can best achieve efficiency, bearing in mind the possible application of specific arbitration rules (by agreement of the parties or as required at the place of arbitration) as well as that of mandatory procedural rules (on account of public order).

1. Autonomy of the arbitral process

The autonomy of the procedural process is a pillar of international arbitration. This is enshrined in the New York Convention (Art. V(1)(d): indeed, if *"the arbitral procedure was not in accordance with the agreement of the parties"*, the award will not be recognized; the UNCITRAL Model Law is also to the same effect as well as national legislations and institutional arbitration rules[1]. The principle of autonomy is particularly palpable in relation to the gathering of evidence. While arbitral rules may vary in the degree of direction they give to parties and arbitrators, they all leave them, on the overall, with much latitude for devising the precise rules that will govern the hearing phase. This does not mean that this aspect of arbitration is of little interest; quite on the contrary, it underscores the importance of customizing the rules for the taking of evidence.

In former times, parties and arbitrators more readily accepted the premise, mostly due to confusion on their part, that the procedural law prevailing at the place of arbitration ought to be applied; fortunately, the practice has swayed in the opposite direction. There is general acceptance today that the *lex arbitri* has gained its independence from the *lex fori*: arbitrators no longer have to demonstrate that they are respectful of rules of universal application such as due process, the right to be heard and the equality of treatment between the parties. Arbitrators are likewise mindful of the specific procedural provisions of the *lex fori* that must be considered to avoid lending arguments to a disgruntled party for contesting the award[2].

If parties to an international arbitration are not likely to be bound by the often intricate procedural features of local judicial systems (although in certain jurisdictions: Luxembourg, Uruguay, for example, local rules ought to be expressly excluded), they must nevertheless in all cases prove their allegations[3]; as a matter of fact, it can be observed that arbitrators increasingly tend to justify their decisions when rejecting the claim of a party, on mere factual points as well as on broader issues, by concluding that he has failed in the discharge of the onus of proof.

2. Oral evidence in international arbitration

The facts can be proven either by written or oral evidence. The merits of each method are discussed in the preceding chapter[4]; live testimony, besides complementing documentary evidence, brings about an indispensable contribution to arbitrators in the pursuit of the truth, be they guided by the civilist tradition of inward or deep-seated belief ("*intime conviction*") or by the common law approach of the balance of evidence.

While the judiciary must comply with rigid national standards in receiving oral evidence, parties and arbitrators are free to develop the rules that are most suitable for each particular case. Parties have an undeniable right to be able to present their case by relying on oral evidence; few will contest that such a prerogative also extends to the possibility of resorting to testimony by witnesses other than the representatives of the parties themselves. Article 20 of the ICC Rules offers an illustration:

"**Article 20**
Establishing the Facts of the Case
.....
2
After studying the written submissions of the parties and all documents relied upon, the arbitral tribunal shall hear the parties together in person if any of them so request or, failing such a request, it may of its own motion decide to hear them.
.....
3
The arbitral tribunal may decide to hear witnesses, experts appointed by the parties or any other person, in the presence of the parties, or in their absence provided they have been duly summoned.
.....
6
The arbitral tribunal may decide the case solely on the documents submitted by the parties unless any of the parties requests a hearing".

The arbitral tribunal must of course remain in full control of the hearings; it must indeed guarantee that the fundamental rights of the parties are safeguarded and that the case proceeds as efficiently and expeditiously as possible towards its conclusion[5]. Although the parties may reach a specific agreement between them and require the arbitral tribunal to conduct the proceedings in a certain manner (of course, the tribunal is not bound to comply with every one of their desiderata), arbitrators will in practice, preferably after having consulted the parties, issue such procedural orders or directions as they find appropriate to govern the hearings. In this connection, the IBA Rules on the Taking of Evidence in International Commercial Arbitration ("IBA Rules") and the UNCITRAL Notes on Organizing Arbitral Proceedings ("UNCITRAL Notes")[6] represent two remarkably useful tools in assisting them.

This chapter will examine, in a chronological order, the various stages and some aspects in relation to the offering of oral evidence in international arbitration.

EVIDENTIARY HEARINGS

1. Who can testify

As a general rule, any person will be admitted to testify without the arbitrators making any differentiation among the various qualities or capacities in which a person may appear: representative of a party, employee or former employee of a party, consultant or expert remunerated by a party or appointed by the Tribunal, spouses and other related persons, "*sachants*" (an outside person who is independently familiar with facts or circumstances relevant to the issues being arbitrated) and "*amicus curiae*": "*In fact, these distinctions are of little significance, as the witnesses themselves generally do not testify under oath and the arbitrators always have the power to assess the weight to be given to their testimony*"[7]. For its part, Article 20-7 of the LCIA Rules indistinctly calls anyone who testifies a "witness"[8].

The facts of the case can be established by all appropriate means, each contributing to fashion the conviction of the arbitrators. They will come naturally to rely on their experience to assess the probative strength of each testimony in the light of the person's relationship with a party, be it direct or indirect, or his interest, financial or sensibility wise, in the case. The statements by a witness will also be balanced against those of other witnesses and even the attitude (aggressivity, signs of sweating, hesitation, looks etc...) of the witnesses will be taken into account in the assessing process.

Internal procedural rules may recognize the status of witness to certain persons only, for instance those who can be sworn or who do not represent a party. It would be most astonishing that such domestic rules could be erected into compelling ones on international arbitrators so that their non-observance would constitute a ground for annulment; however, arbitrators should be attentive to the legal requirements at the place of arbitration since it is the jurisdiction where annulment proceedings can be initiated.

Whereas Article 20(3) of the ICC Rules does not mandate the hearing of "*witnesses*" or "*any other person*", Article 20(2) of the same Rules provides a right for a "*party*" to be heard if he so requests. Although the ICC Rules distinguish between the representative of a party and a witness, they do not purport to lay down any kind of standard which the arbitrators would be required to apply in assessing the probative value of their evidence. Hearings of parties' representatives and of any other person whose testimony is relevant, are normal occurrences in international arbitral proceedings, no matter under what rules they are conducted[9]. An arbitrator, however, refused to consider as a *witness statement* the written declaration filed by the legal representative of a party since the latter could not be considered as a witness; the German nationality of the arbitrator could explain why he reached such a decision[10].

Article 4(2) of the IBA Rules reflects the current practice in this regard: "*Any person may present evidence as a witness, including a Party or a Party's officer, employee or other representative.*" For their part, albeit after some debate, the UNCITRAL Notes infer no restriction as to the persons who can be heard; the Notes merely draw the arbitrators' attention to the particularities that may be encountered in national legislations, especially as to the manner in which the testimony of certain persons can be received[11].

While any person can be called upon to testify, some concerns have been raised about the possible incidence of professional or ethical norms that may govern legal advisors of international organizations in connection with their appearance before arbitral tribunals in particular if called upon (*e.g.* as party-appointed expert) to interpret the provisions of an investment treaty pursuant to which an arbitration was commenced. On the assumption that the international civil servant comes forward after being allowed by its organization to depose or is prepared to accept the risk of reprove by the organization, it would seem that a tribunal should not refuse to hear him; the tribunal's uncurtailed authority to draw inferences in assessing the value of the evidence will offset arguable indelicacies that the non-observance of the duty of impartiality and neutrality inherent to the international civil service may entail. Arbitrators should not be expected to be the guardians of institutional interests. Similar questions could arise in respect to a person who acted as arbitrator or counsel in a case involving one or both parties or related issues. Of course, in line with Article 9.2(b) of the IBA Rules, arbitrators should remain circumspect and be attentive to political reality in such situations to avoid a backlash against the universal acceptance that international arbitration has gained over the years.

In January 2001, in the Methanex Corporation vs United States of America, an Arbitration under Chapter 11 of the North American Free Trade Agreement and the UNCITRAL Rules, the tribunal considered entertaining written submissions from interested third-parties. This tribunal then issued guidelines on 30 December 2003 for such submissions and two *amicus curiae* briefs were produced. The direction from the tribunal refers to written submissions from "*any non-disputing party that is a person of a Party, or that has a significant presence in the territory of a Party*"; such an initiative could also prove of benefit in certain international arbitration proceedings when issues of wider interest are raised, subject of course to the protection flowing notably from the private foundation of the arbitral process, to which parties are entitled.

Article 20(3) of the ICC Rules contemplates that arbitrators may decide to hear "*any other person*"; such "other person" could include a "*friend of the court*" who, by definition, does not need to be compelled to appear, which power arbitrators lack anyhow. In the Methanex case, the tribunal based its jurisdiction to accept *amicus curiae* briefs on its general power to manage the arbitral proceedings[12].

Of course, if it is a party that requests the hearing of a certain person as *amicus curiae*, the tribunal will be careful of the semantics; it could be a disguised application for the appointment of an expert.

Whereas judges are invested with the power to order any person within their jurisdiction to appear before them, arbitrators, without the assistance of the judiciary (when available), cannot coerce witnesses to testify before them. On the other hand, arbitrators can receive, in principle, the deposition of any person as compared to the judiciary which remains bound to act within the limits set by its own municipal laws. For instance, a Quebec court cannot hear, under pain of the nullity of the deposition, a person that has not solemnly affirmed to tell the truth[13]. In certain legislations, spousal or family relationships and interest can constitute grounds for objection to the appearance of a person; such objection may only go, under some other legislations, to the credibility of the witness as it would be the case in arbitration.

In a nutshell, the lack of *imperium* of the arbitrators can be said to be compensated by the more extensive freedom they enjoy as to which persons they can hear.

2. Selection and calling of witnesses

Based on the premise that each party has to prove its case, it rests upon him to identify and present the witnesses upon whose evidence he intends to rely. This aspect is inherent to the burden of proof rule. It implies that each party is responsible for insuring the presence of his witnesses at the hearing; different situations will arise.

Unless they are officers or employees of a corporate party, financial compensation will have to be arranged to cover the costs of coming to the hearing. Some witnesses, in particular consultants, will insist on being paid for their time, including preparation, whereas others, such as former employees, may have to obtain the authorization of their current employer. In some instances, a party may wish to call persons unrelated to the case as such but who can testify, for instance, as to the difficulties encountered in the country where the project being arbitrated took place or as to parallel sales in a given market.

A difficult issue often arises in practice in relation to the timing of the disclosure of the name, status and address of witnesses. There are two schools of thought: arbitrators who direct parties to state in their briefs which persons will be called upon to testify in support of allegations intended to be proven by oral evidence while others only require the parties to reveal the identity of their witnesses some time prior to the hearing. Bearing in mind that a party may not always be in a position to know definitively which person will be best suited to testify on a given aspect, especially when all the briefs have not yet been produced, or which person will be available when the hearing comes, let alone a party's fear that the adverse party may either contact his witnesses with a view to influencing them or gain a better understanding of his strategy, it may be sufficient for a party to indicate in his briefs which allegations will be proven by oral evidence and disclose the names of the witnesses later.

Normally, the Terms of Reference or a procedural order will require the parties to provide the name, the exact address and the subject matter of the testimony of each intended witness by a certain time before the hearing, unless full witness statements have been agreed upon[14]. The UNCITRAL Arbitration Rules (Art. 25(2)) as well as the EDF Conciliation and Arbitration Rules (Art. 26(2)) stipulate a minimum delay of fifteen days before the hearing for disclosing the names of witnesses[15]. The same minimum notice period is provided for in the new January 1, 2004 Swiss Rules of International Arbitration at Article 25(2). It would be reasonable that such disclosure takes place as soon as possible after the last brief has been filed (e.g. two weeks) and to allow for the maximum period of time possible before the hearing. Claimant should first file his list and then respondent with sufficient time allowed for claimant, whenever possible, to permit modifying his list or adding new names, should it be warranted, as rebuttal witnesses.

There should be a general understanding that once the arbitral tribunal has confirmed who will appear at the hearing, the party must ensure that the announced witnesses will in fact be present. Indeed, the opposite party will most likely have planned certain aspects of the presentation of his evidence according to which witnesses have been called by the other side. The tribunal itself may be looking forward to hearing a particular witness or question him.

It is unfair for a party to cancel at the last minute, often at the start of the hearing, the presence of an announced witness; if a party no longer wishes to produce a witness named on his list, he should nonetheless arrange for his presence at the hearing so that the other side has an opportunity to question him should he desire[16]. Otherwise, the tribunal may draw inferences against the party who did not make the witness available unless valid reasons can be given. As soon as difficulties arise in this connection, the tribunal must accommodate the situation after having solicited the views of the parties and ensuring fairness and equality of treatment between the parties. Except in very exceptional circumstances and in any event with the other party's acquiescence, no eleventh hour witness should be tolerated; this is tantamount to a violation of due process.

No matter which approach is adopted (disclosure of names of witnesses in the briefs or at some point of time before the planned evidentiary hearing), arbitrators must be vigilant in confirming the list of those persons who will introduce evidence at the hearing; the issuance of a final list by the tribunal may prove a difficult, if not time-consuming exercise. In a normal arbitration, each party will be represented by one representative and will call two or three fact witnesses and perhaps one expert-witness; no particular issue will arise in such a case but the context may dictate otherwise.

The tribunal may wish to hear a person whose testimony has not yet been offered (IBA Rules, Article 4.11; ICC Rules, Article 20(3)); this may require early action and it could raise questions in the parties' mind. Another situation is when a party needs the assistance of the tribunal in securing the presence of a witness who will not appear spontaneously such as an employee of a certifying or consulting firm that conducted an investigation in relation to the project being submitted to arbitration. An official invitation letter from the arbitral tribunal may suffice. The party who sought his testimony would normally advance his costs but it may not be the case if the witness is seen as neutral and independent from the parties' respective position. Under US federal law and most State laws, arbitrators may issue themselves subpoenas compelling any person within the jurisdiction to attend before them as witness[17]; such a practice is unknown in most civilist jurisdictions.

In some cases, rogatory commissions can be organized, normally with the assistance of the courts at the place of arbitration and those at the place of residence of the witness[18]. A "commission" is issued by the local court to a foreign court that will summon an individual within his jurisdiction to depose.

For obvious reasons of timing and efficiency, the party seeking a commission will liaise with the tribunal which may even decide to apply himself to the local courts to initiate the process. Once the witness, usually a third-party, knows that he can be coerced by his own courts to give evidence, he is likely to accept to testify before a local court reporter and local counsel (if counsel involved in the case do not do it themselves). The arbitrator will issue guidelines for such examination abroad and sometimes the testimony will be given in the form of answers to an agreed list of questions.

There is a case (unreported) of an ICC tribunal (sitting in Geneva) which agreed to hear, in the presence of the parties and their counsel, the evidence of a witness (an ex-employee of a party) at his place of residence (France); considering the expenses involved, an issue of cost may have to be settled in such situations. For the sake of completeness, arbitrators can consider the appropriateness of resorting to other methods to receive evidence. Although there is no unanimous view as to whether the evidence may be taken by one arbitrator instead of by the entire tribunal[19], it can indeed prove useful in a limited number of cases and provided the basic guarantees of the parties (access to the evidence and right to question the witness) are preserved, to put in the record evidence that might otherwise be difficult if not impossible to gather by reason of time, costs, non-availability of arbitrators, fastidious collection of evidence especially if of a corroborating nature only etc...

With the considerable improvement of the quality of video-conferencing[20], arbitrators should no longer hesitate to resort, at least to propose it to the parties, to such a means of collecting oral evidence from witnesses who would otherwise hardly be, if at all, available to testify. If on-line arbitration as an overall process still has to be accepted as an efficient and confidential way of conducting arbitration, high quality video-conferencing can practically be as effective as an examination and cross-examination conducted live.

There is general agreement that an arbitral tribunal is not obliged to hear all the evidence offered especially when it becomes repetitive and irrelevant. It becomes however more perilous to refuse to hear one or more witnesses altogether. Parties, especially from common law jurisdictions, will envisage relatively prolonged hearings on account of the number of witnesses they intend to call. Discussions often take place between the parties and the arbitrators to fix the proper length of the oral evidence phase. Each party must have a reasonable opportunity to present his case; this is entrenched in the parties' fundamental right of due process. Nonetheless, the arbitrators, who remain in charge of the hearings, may consider that certain testimonies will be superfluous, impractical to obtain without disrupting the timetable of the proceedings, disruptive of the equality between the parties, etc...; the arbitrators can therefore in certain circumstances refuse to hear witnesses without denying a party's right to due process[21]. In order to illustrate the point, take the case of a party that insists, as essential to his defence, that the former wife and business partner of the owner of the corporate party, now living in the opposite hemisphere, be called to testify in a dispute now involving the new wife and business partner: the arbitrator's discernment will not be betrayed by this disguised attempt to put undue stress on the adversary. Tense discussions sometimes take place within the panel in this respect especially where it is composed of arbitrators from different legal traditions. Can the arbitrators limit the number of representatives of a party as they may do with witnesses, in trying to achieve a certain equality between the parties?

Other vital aspects of oral evidence are dealt with elsewhere: preparation of witnesses [Chapter 3, page 55] and witness statements [Chapter 4, page 65]; both steps, which precede the formal evidentiary hearing, are meant to streamline the collection of oral evidence. Recourse to pre-hearing discovery may also avail as a useful tool especially when counsel are both from a legal tradition that admits such a procedure, but not necessarily so[22]. Counsel would normally submit to the tribunal the arrangements and schedule they will have worked out between themselves; the tribunal, after reviewing, modifying and completing the proposal, will issue a procedural order to allow for such discovery. The entire transcript of the discovery and all the exhibits produced at that time will become part of the record of the arbitration unless the tribunal decide that testimony needs to be reintroduced at the hearing. In any event, this procedure should allow the parties at the hearing to limit their presentation to the essential points, leaving the arbitrator free to base his reasoning on, or complete it with the pre-hearing oral evidence filed. The appearance of non-key witnesses may be dispensed with, the transcript of their sworn testimony being sufficient since both parties participated in the discovery. Difficulties in the taking of the depositions during discovery will be settled by the arbitral tribunal as they arise.

3. Organizing the evidentiary hearing

The jurisdictional function of the arbitrator is necessarily complemented by his managerial role. The arbitration is as good as the arbitrator is, but the failure to control the proceedings can be disastrous for the arbitral process. A lawyer pleading before his own court will instinctively follow the procedural rules that he has been taught and which all the other members of the same bar also embrace. The local judges evolve within the same system and will ensure compliance with the procedural rules that the legislator or other competent authority in their jurisdiction have enacted. There is no such set of standard rules for counsel to follow when appearing before international arbitration panels; no matter how well-versed counsel may be in the applicable substantive rules of law, he will often not be adequately armed to find his way through vague or lacking procedural rules before an arbitral tribunal.

■ Early issuance of customized procedural rules

Contrary to defenders before municipal courts, counsel in international arbitration must be guided and directed throughout the arbitral process. Counsel are rarely from the same jurisdiction; they practice their art very differently. It must be realized that the most taxing hurdle for lawyers in international arbitration is to leave outside the hearing room their own procedure coloured spectacles; if they do not, they will likely become critical of the proceedings and miss opportunities in the representation of their client. On the other hand, arbitrators must fully apprehend that they are expected to "enact" the rules that will govern the proceedings; like counsel appearing before them, they must leave behind their own national procedure. Arbitrators must devise appropriate rules to fill in the quasi-procedural void in international arbitration. The UNCITRAL Notes are useful tools to assist them in adopting procedural rules that will respect the sensitivity and legal culture of each party. This is particularly true when it comes to the organization of the evidentiary hearings. The IBA Rules are to be saluted for inspiring some harmonization for the taking of evidence in international arbitration; yet, it can be observed generally that the most experienced arbitrators will issue detailed directions to insure that counsel on both sides will have, as early as possible, the same understanding of the "rules of the game"[23].

The arbitrator is well advised to consider some of the main features of the hearings at the initial stage of the proceedings, notably during the organizational phase of the arbitration when the arbitrators, counsel and the representatives of the parties can meet together. The exchange of views will enable the tribunal to fix a provisional timetable as envisaged in the new Article 18(4) of the ICC Rules. Once the need for an evidentiary hearing has been established, dates can be set aside usually with some reserved days as it is usually impossible to fix, at that time, the precise schedule of the hearing; this gives sufficient head time to ensure the availability of all those who will participate in the hearings or to reschedule the hearings with the least disruptions (e.g. as to the venue). The parties can be directed to indicate in the briefs which allegations will be proven by oral evidence and, when possible, the identity of the witnesses; the manner and the order for taking oral evidence can be decided upon as well as the need for a verbatim record and interpretation. Parties can also agree on the introduction of written statements. More and more procedural orders indicate that the IBA Rules will be kept in mind by the tribunal during the proceedings or that they are adopted, in whole or in part, to govern them.

At the close of the exchange of briefs, i.e. hopefully with an adequate lead time of a good two months before the hearing, the tribunal, in consultation with the parties, will prepare one or more procedural order(s) specifically dealing with the organization of the presentation of testimony. Besides the venue of the hearings which can be conducted at any appropriate location (e.g. Art. 14(2) of the ICC Rules), several matters will be covered.

■ List of witnesses and subject matter of their testimony

As far ahead as possible before the hearing dates, parties are requested to confirm the identity of the persons, with full particulars including a CV and an identity picture, who will be produced to give evidence. The subject matter of their testimony will be indicated in sufficient detail and with reference to the parts of the briefs to which their testimony will relate; an indication of the expected duration of their testimony should be provided. Time permitting, the claimant party will send in his list first, then the respondent followed by an opportunity for claimant to submit a list of rebuttal witnesses. With this information in hand, the tribunal will put together, for the parties' further comments, if matters are not entirely settled, the procedural order setting forth the order and the duration of the presentation by each witness allowing for possible opening and possibly closing statements by counsel as well as for questioning time by the other party and sometimes accommodating the constraints of particular witnesses (travel schedule, limited availability...).

If witness statements have been filed, they will normally serve as direct testimony, the other party then proceeding forthwith with his own questioning. Professor Claude Reymond was one of the first to voice that American styled "examination" and "cross-examination" have no place in international commercial arbitration. This was recognized by the members of the Working Party in charge of drafting the IBA Rules: they stayed away from these notions and favoured the terms "direct testimony" and "question" the witnesses.

At the time of putting together the list of persons that will be heard, there may be a need for exchanges of views with the parties concerning the duration, the relevance and the possible redundancy of the testimony, in the light of the overall reserved time for the evidentiary hearing. As Jan Paulsson[24] puts it: "*... it may be possible to posit... the following 'good housekeeping rules' .... As for witnesses called by a party, ... the arbitrator should have full authority to limit their appearance on the grounds of irrelevance or redundance ... including the right to limit or deny the right of a party to examine, cross-examine or re-examine a witness if he determines it to be unlikely to serve any further relevant purpose*". This is always a delicate exercise to balance between the efficiency of the proceedings, time and costs wise, and the principle of due process a violation of which could frustrate the award[25]. Should the parties' wishes not be fully taken into account at that time, it remains possible for the tribunal, once conversant with the evidence already before it, to resume the hearing at a later date if needs be.

The built-in flexibility of the arbitral process allows arbitrators to adapt and complete any guidelines for the presentation of the evidence. This flexibility will be used at the start or, as required, in the course of the hearings. For instance, witness conferencing can be envisaged[26] or the *confronto* method of tandem witness examination resorted to. This latter method provides for two witnesses to be heard simultaneously; they are then invited to explain the reasons for possible differences[27]. Depending on their legal training, the arbitrators may wish to ask questions first leaving less time to counsel; however, some counsel who have already prepared their presentation, may not be content with this approach.

■ Transcript, interpretation

In most international arbitration proceedings, the deposition of witnesses will be recorded verbatim; nowadays, civil law tribunals will be inclined to have stenographic records of the hearing just as much as common law ones[28]. Likewise, translation/interpretation will be required in many instances. At the organizational stage, it is wise to visit all the questions that this raises. The arrangements as a general rule are made by the arbitrator or the chairman. Care must be taken of certain specifics. The advances on the arbitration costs may or may not have taken the related expenses into account; some adjustments may be needed or a special deposit paid.

A party may insist on transcript delivery the same day; if the other does not want to pay the added cost, is it proper for the tribunal to allow the requesting party to do so at its own expense at the risk of violating the equality between the parties? The transcript made only by one party will not avail as proof[29]. The parties may agree to have live note recording; it is suggested that they should make the arrangements themselves especially if the arbitrators are not familiar with this system. With respect to transcripts, it is wise to provide for a certain time limit for the parties to indicate corrections; of course, corrections must relate to what the witness actually said and not to what he intended to say. As one author noted[30], the lack of recording is not per se a cause of nullity of the proceedings but that *"this may be the case whenever absence of record prevents a decisive point being established with certainty"*. In 1999, the Paris Court of Appeal decided that the absence of a full transcript of the oral evidence given in an arbitration did not, in itself, violate due process[31].

Interpretation may be consecutive or simultaneous; again there will be a difference in costs. If all the witnesses can express themselves in the language of the arbitration, but some are not confident in their level of sufficiency, who should advance the costs for the individual assistance required? Will these form part of the costs of arbitration independently of who advanced the expenses? What will be the interaction of the private interpretation with the recording being made in the language of the arbitration? Would a party be right in objecting (e.g. for having to call in an additional counsel) if the tribunal were to allow arguments on points of law in the language of the substantive law notwithstanding the official language of the arbitration?

■ Presence or exclusion of witnesses

Unless the parties agree otherwise, hearings shall be held in camera; Article 25(4) of the Swiss Rules of International Arbitration goes on to state that the arbitrator may require the retirement of any witness during the testimony of other witnesses. Of course, representatives of the parties have a right to be present throughout the hearing even if they are to be called to testify (e.g. Art. 20(3) ICC Rules).

Experts, whether party-appointed or named by the tribunal, will, as a rule, stay in the room throughout the hearings and their testimony will generally come last. Their observations and conclusions can thus relate more closely to the actual events and circumstances of the case and they will be in position to highlight and clarify certain aspects of their report for the benefit of the tribunal.

In order to avoid antagonizing one of the parties, if not the two of them, the tribunal should not wait until the actual hearings commence to canvass the parties' desiderata; this topic should be covered at the time the organizational procedural order is issued. Since separate questioning is likely to increase the time for the hearing[32], the tribunal will remain mindful of the planned schedule. There seems to be no set rule in this connection[33] although the practice is still influenced, albeit to a lesser degree as the arbitral process gains in independence, by the judiciary systems of the arbitrators and counsel. The parties may agree that witnesses be present at all times by deference to those who may have to wait in hotel rooms until their turn comes[34]. The tribunal may also deal in the procedural order with the possibility or interdiction for witnesses who have not yet testified to review transcripts when they are ready at the end of each day; likewise, when a testimony is suspended (e.g. lunch break,...), the witness should be instructed not to discuss his evidence or performance with anyone.

In large project arbitrations, the tendency seems to be that witnesses will testify in the presence of each others; they generally have worked together for a number of months or years and normally have learned to appreciate, if not to know one another. The discipline that ought to prevail at the hearings is not threatened in such cases. However, if feelings have been exasperated during the parties' working relationship, especially when founded on a more personal association (*"intuitus personae"*), it may become demanding to achieve a smooth control over hearings possibly plagued with outbursts and unsolicited interventions.

In deciding whether to exclude witnesses or not, the arbitrator will be guided by his quest for the truth in establishing the facts. In the light of the context of the dispute as described in the briefs, the arbitrator has to opt for the approach that will be the more amenable for the witness to speak out freely and to the point: a person testifying in the presence of someone whom he came to loathe will tend to present an exaggerated version of certain facts while former work colleagues, especially if from the same trade, will be more inclined to depose in an objective manner as they stand to be immediately corrected. In case of exclusion, a witness who has testified may want to remain in the room; this will be allowed as a rule but provided he is not called again to give evidence to avoid giving him an undue advantage.

4. Giving evidence at evidentiary hearings

■ Introduction

Little assistance is found in arbitration rules as to the manner in which oral evidence is to be produced in front of arbitral tribunals. This intended void illustrates at best the built-in flexibility of the international arbitral process. The arbitrator's role is crucial at that stage of the proceedings to ensure maximum efficiency of the fact-finding phase. Again, arbitrators can find much comfort in the IBA Rules. In the quasi-absence of express safeguards, arbitrators must constantly keep in mind the fundamental principles of "due process" and of the "equal treatment of the parties". The weight of the evidence can only be fairly assessed if these principles are not violated.

Authors have been prolific in comparing the advantages and disadvantages of the civil law regime and of the common law system for receiving oral evidence in international arbitration[35]. Indeed, there is no better fertile soil than international arbitration to test the merits of the two approaches. However, experienced arbitrators have not shown much concern over such analysis in the past few years since they gradually came to apply the best of the two systems, melting them with relative ease in practice. The IBA Rules, which were developed by practitioners originating form various legal traditions, are a modern example of harmonization in the field of adducing evidence in international commercial arbitration; parties, counsel and arbitrators alike, wherever they are from, can follow these Rules without hurting their inner sense of justice. True multicultural arbitrators must be preferred to those whose only claim to fame is the mastering of the civilist and common law traditions.

Much has been written on the taking of evidence and it is not intended here to summarize the literature on the subject. With respect to administering the oaths before an individual testifies, reference is made to the developments in Chapter 6, page 87. Rather, this section will address some singular issues that can arise in the course of the evidentiary hearings no matter how well planned they have been.

■ Witness assisted by counsel

Parties are generally assisted by advisers; can a witness, during his testimony, be advised by a lawyer? An engineer that has designed a plant over which an arbitration is proceeding between the owner and the contractor, may condition his appearance on being accompanied by his lawyer since a separate action is being threatened against him by the contractor: is his lawyer welcome at the hearing? Maybe not but provided the testimony is not interfered with or influenced, the witness will have some assurances that he will be able to formulate his responses in a manner that will not disserve him later on. Despite the duty of confidentiality associated with arbitration, the transcript (or extracts) of evidence given before an arbitral panel may very well get filed in a court case; once produced, there is not much that can be done to reverse the situation. If the tribunal summoned the witness who is assisted by counsel, should the costs of the witness' lawyer be part of the costs of arbitration?

■ Reading from documents that are not exhibits

Witnesses are handed the exhibits in relation to which they are testifying. However, a witness can pull out his diary or excerpts from it or walk to the witness stand with notes that he had prepared to help him depose. Most of the time, even counsel of the party producing the witness will have been unaware that this would happen; of course, opposite counsel will immediately ask that the documents in question be turned in the record. In exercising his control, the arbitrator will enquire as to the nature of the notes or document and decide upon their production. In most instances, they will be personal notes of the witness and production will not be ordered. Conversely, if the document is directly relevant to the matter in dispute, it should be filed in the record and be subjected to examination by the other side. If the arbitrator is not able to rule on the basis of the explanations provided by the witness as to the nature and import of the document, then he should inspect it and, as warranted, afford the opposing party the opportunity to inspect it as well[36].

Should the fact that the document was obtained or copied from the confidential files of one of the parties or even from those of a third-party affect the ruling? Can the witness, having procured the document fraudulently on the eve of his dismissal or lay-off, nonetheless comment on the document in his testimony? Should his testimony be struck off the record if the fraudulent document on which it is based is revealed afterwards? Arbitrators are not restricted in this area by national laws in the way that the judiciary is; furthermore local laws differ and some, as in France, admit a greater latitude than in common law jurisdictions[37]; even in England, each case needs to be considered on its merits and the requirements of procedural fairness are not cast in stone when it comes to the desirability of producing raided documents before an unrelated authority[38]. Finally, admissibility of evidence in international arbitration is not as strict as before domestic courts, there being no national interest to protect[39]. In his assessment of the probative value of the evidence, the arbitrator will take into account all the circumstances. He will not allow evidence if there are compelling ethical rules, as he may determine, that dictate such a decision (e.g. Art. 9.2(b) of the IBA Rules).

■ Allowing unequal time

In preparing the schedule for the hearing, the arbitrator will normally allot equal time to both sides; this reflects the rule that the parties must be treated with equal fairness. But should this always be the case? If the parties announce disproportionate lists of witnesses, then an equal division of time would not be fair. However, if the arbitrator detects that one party is prevented from calling a "normal" number of persons on account of the high expenses involved or of his inability to reach or convince potential witnesses to come (e.g. a lasting dispute and former employees), then he may talk the other side into not bringing all the intended witnesses to reinstate some kind of balance. There can also be circumstances where one party legitimately needs more time[40]. The time for the consecutive interpretation of the witnesses of a party should be deducted in computing the duration of the testimony on each side.

■ Testimony by counsel

Of course, most procedural rules before courts and bar regulations forbid counsel assisting a party in a case, to give evidence in the same matter; in common law procedure, the judge will cut short explanations given by counsel if they are akin to testimony. In international arbitration, there is no such rule.

Arbitrators can freely ask a counsel to summarize or relate facts for the record instead of going through a laborious question-answer process to get to the same result; counsel may present some of the factual background that he has been made aware of in preparing the case and assembling the exhibits; of course, this is done in front of the witness so that the opposite party can question the witness directly. This pragmatic approach is particularly time-saving when the witness is not conversant with the language of the arbitration, has difficulty in clearly and concisely describing the facts or does not understand the point on which he is asked to testify. There is no difference here, it seems, with witness statements that have been carefully prepared by counsel; in the same way that the witness will simply sign his statement (presumably after having read it), the witness listening to counsel answering a question can just nod his acceptance of the verbal statement just made. The witness can immediately be questioned by the other side the same way opposite counsel can cross-examine the signatory of a statement availing as direct examination.

■ Taking pictures and filming

Credibility is paramount in assessing the weight of evidence. This ingredient is not only distilled through what the witness say but also through his whole conduct. Unconsciously, arbitrators may subject, without anyone knowing, the individual testifying before them to some kind of profiling; it is often said that gesture may lead to some inference that a witness is lying or withholding part of the story. Unfortunately, the perception that the arbitrator may have forged for himself during a witness' presentation will vanish over time; the demeanour of witnesses does not transpire in transcripts. It is always helpful for the members of a panel to review together the attitude of the various witnesses in the presentation of their evidence; however, memories vanish with the passage of time. A solution may be found by having a member of the tribunal (preferably the secretary of the tribunal or an assistant who could come for that purpose and why not a professional) taking some pictures of the witnesses and, perhaps, of the setting generally; more daring arbitrators may even make short videos of some brief sequences of the testimony. Such measure can be introduced with finesse so as not to hurt any feelings. For instance, the matter could be evoked during the first organizational meeting and be made part of the ensuing order. When the hearing arrives, the matter will have been noted and no difficulty should arise.

Parties will sometimes bring into the hearing room some kind of demonstrative evidence to assist the arbitrators in gaining a better understanding, for instance a scale model of a power plant; a tridimensional view will definitely be of assistance. Likewise, a witness will back up his oral evidence by going to the "white board" (it can immediately produce a photocopy of the drawings or other sketches which a traditional "black board" cannot do). Technical explanations will thus be easier for the panel to follow. However, the usefulness of the exercise will have totally disappeared at the time of reading the transcript: the witness draws a line with his pointer from that point to this point. In complex technical or construction matters, such demonstrations by witnesses and in particular experts are not a rare occurrence. Here again, oral testimony given with the help of a drawing board or the placing of a model in the hearing room would retain its benefit if they could be viewed by the arbitrators during their deliberation, that is if a video has been made of the relevant parts of the testimony. One word of caution: if video is to be made of some of the presentations, and not only of the witnesses during a few seconds, hiring a technician is recommended so as not to overburden the panel.

END NOTES

1 The New York Convention on the Recognition and Enforcement of Foreign Arbitral Awards, adopted on June 10, 1958 by the General Assembly of the United Nations; UNCITRAL Model Law on International Commercial Arbitration adopted on June 21, 1985 by the United Commission on International Trade Law: Art. 19(1): "... *[s]ubject to the provisions of this Law, the parties are free to agree on the procedure to be followed by the arbitral tribunal in conducting the proceedings*". Some examples of national legislations: Netherlands Code of Civil Procedure, Art. 1036, French New Code of Civil Procedure, Art. 1494, Algerian Decree Law of April 23, 1993 and of institutional rules: ICC Rules of Arbitration in force from 1 January 1998, Art. 15(1); AAA International Arbitration Rules (7 April 1997 edition), Art. 16(1) & (2); LCIA Arbitration Rules in force from January 1, 1998, Art. 14(1).

2 See E. Gaillard, "Arbitrage commercial international", J.-Cl. Droit international, Fascicule 586-8-1 ou Procédure civile, Fascicule 1067, 1994, pp. 2-9.

3 Redfern, Reymond et al. The Standards and Burden of Proof in International Arbitration, Arb. Int., Vol. 10, 1994, No. 3, p. 317; M. Rubino-Sammartano, International Arbitration, Law and Practice, 2nd ed., Kluwer Law International, 2001, pp. 653-656; Swiss Rules of International Arbitration, January 2004, Art. 24-25.

4 Antonias Dimolitsa, [Chapter 1, p. 11, supra].

5 ICC Rules (1998), Art. 21(3), AAA Arbitration Rules (1997), Art. 20(4), LCIA Rules (1998), Art. 19.5, ICSID Rules (1984), Art. 14; Delvolvé Rouche Pointon, French Arbitration Law and Practice, Kluwer Law International, 2003, pp. 117-118.

6 IBA Rules of Evidence on the Taking of Evidence in International Commercial Arbitration, adopted by a resolution of the IBA Council on 1 June 1999, International Bar Association; UNCITRAL Notes on Organizing Arbitral Proceedings, United Nations, Vienna, 1996.

7 E. Gaillard and J. Savage (eds), Fouchard Gaillard Goldman on International Commercial Arbitration, Kluwer Law International, 1999, p. 699.

8 Article 20-7 of the LCIA Rules: *"Any individual intending to testify to the arbitral tribunal on any issue of fact or expertise shall be treated as a witness under these Rules notwithstanding that the individual is a party to the arbitration or was or is an officer, employee or shareholder of any party".*

9 See for instance, in the case of the ICC Rules: Y. Derains and E. Schwartz, A Guide to the New ICC Rules of Arbitration, Kluwer Law International, 1998, pp. 254-257.

10 D. Hascher, Collection of Procedural Decisions in ICC Arbitrations 1993-1996, Kluwer Law International and ICC Publishing SA, 1997, pp. 96-102, commenting a decision rendered in case 7319 (at p. 102: "*Placé devant le problème de la distinction entre témoin et représentant d'une partie, l'arbitre, plutôt que, comme en l'espèce, décider entre la voie de l'enquête ou celle de l'audition des parties, pourrait de préférence indiquer aux parties (et à leurs conseils) qu'il entendra toute personne susceptible d'apporter un éclaircissement sur l'affaire*").

11 "Questions Concerning the Desirability and Text of the UNCITRAL Project to Improve Planning of Arbitral Proceedings", ICCA Congress Series No. 7, op. cit., pp. 173-196. At p. 186, Howard M. Holtzmann summarizes the discussions that led to the adoption of Annotation 15(e) "*Hearing representatives of a party*": "*Consider whether persons interested in the outcome of the case can testify as witnesses (e.g. can an executive employed by a company testify as a witness concerning a transaction in which he participated?). If interested persons cannot be witnesses, consider ground rules for determining what persons, or categories of persons, have sufficient interest so that they will not be admitted as witnesses (e.g., persons who are shareholders? persons who are directors or managers? persons who are retired and receive a pension? Or any employee regardless of status?). If interested persons cannot be witnesses, consider whether and if so how, the tribunal will receive information from them*". Compare with the final text of Annotation 15(e): "*According to some legal systems, certain persons affiliated with a party may only be heard as representatives of the party but not as witnesses. In such a case, it may be necessary to consider ground rules for determining which persons may not testify as witnesses (e.g. certain executives, employees or agents) and for hearing statements of those persons and for questioning them*".

12 For a scholarly analysis of the arbitrators' power to organize the procedure under civil law and common law, see P. Mayer, "Le pouvoir des arbitres de régler la procédure: une analyse comparative des systèmes de civil law et de common law", Revue de l'Arbitrage, 1995, No. 2, pp. 163-184.

13 Article 299 of the Quebec Code of Civil Procedure.

14 M.E. Schneider, ASA Bulletin No. 2, 1993, pp. 302-332, in particular document 1, section 3-6 at p. 315, document 8, section 4-1 at p. 320; see also M. Bühler and C. Dorgan, "Witness Testimony pursuant to the 1999 IBA Rules of Evidence in International Commercial Arbitration – Novel or Tested Standards?", Journal of International Arbitration, Vol. 17, No. 1, 2000, Section IV B.

15 UNCITRAL Arbitration Rules, 1976, promulgated by UN resolution 31/98 and adopted by the Assembly of the United Nations on December 15, 1976; Procedural Rules on Conciliation and Arbitration of Contracts Financed by the European Development Fund, Annex V to Decision No. 3/90 of the ACP-EEC Council of Ministers of 29 March 1990.

16 See G. Lörcher, Improving Procedures for Oral and Written Witness Testimony, ICCA Congress Series No. 7, Planning Efficient Arbitration Proceedings, p. 149: *"Therefore, unless both parties renounce the hearing of a witness or oral testimony altogether, oral testimony should be heard if it is offered in points which are material to deciding the case".*

17 Section 7 of the United States Arbitration Act, 9 USC, and the relevant enabling legislations whereby the Uniform Arbitration Act was incorporated in various states; Sulzer v Somagec et al, Court of Appeal, Paris, November 27, 1987, Rev. arb. 1989, p. 62, cited by M. Rubino-Sammartano, op. cit., p. 685.

18 Generally see Evidence in International Arbitration Proceedings, AIJA Law Library Series, Edition AIJA and Graham & Trotman / Martinus Nijhoff, 1994, especially the national reports dealing with Question 4.2 "Obligation to Appear". See e.g. in this connection the references given by M. Buhler and C. Dorgan in footnote 64 (footnote 14 supra), by Y. Derains and E. Schwartz, in footnote 579 (footnote 9 supra); see also M. Rubino-Sammartano, op.cit., at pp. 693-695; J.-F. Poudret and S. Besson, "Droit comparé de l'arbitrage international", Bruylant, 2002, pp. 597-602; A. Redfern and M. Hunter, Law and Practice of International Commercial Arbitration, Sweet & Maxwell, 3rd Edition, 1999, para. 6-80; Conférence de M. Rouhette, Rev. Arb. 1973, pp. 247-248; G.B. Born, International Commercial Arbitration in the United States, Commentary & Materials, Kluwer, 1994, pp. 855-861.

19 See comments in M. Rubino-Sammartano, op.cit., at pp. 665-666.

20 E. Schäfer, "Videoconferencing in Arbitration", ICC International Court of Arbitration Bulletin, Spring 2003, Vol. 14/No. 1, pp. 35-45.

21 Y. Derains and E. Schwartz, op. cit., at p. 256: this has been confirmed in both France and England, see the references mentioned. M. Rubino-Sammartano, op. cit., pp. 658-659 is of the opinion that the practice of limiting the number of witnesses must not be approved especially with a view to saving time; he argues that, save in special situations, the arbitrator is not in a position to assess, before hearing the witnesses, whether one or more of them will be necessary. A. Redfern and M. Hunter, op. cit., at para. 6-103, state: "*The trend in international arbitration is toward shorter hearings with greater reliance upon documentary evidence. This is a necessary step in the interests of economy of time and costs...*".

22 An arbitral tribunal composed of three arbitrators from a continental tradition choose a method reminiscent of discovery in ICC case No. 7170, 1992, commented in Journal du Droit International, 1993, at pp. 1082-1084.

23 A Procedural Order rendered in ICC case no 7314 on 17 February 1994 gives a good illustration (almost a manual) of detailed directives to the parties in preparation to an evidentiary hearing; reproduced with a commentary in Journal du Droit International (Clunet), 1996, No. 1, at pp. 1045-1049.

24 International Council for Commercial Arbitration Congress Series No. 7, Planning Efficient Arbitration Proceedings, at p. 119.

25 Iron Ore Company of Canada vs Argonaut Shipping, Inc., US District Court, Southern District of New York, 9 September 1985, commented in Yearbook Commercial Arbitration, Vol. XII – 1987, Kluwer, at pp. 173-176. Arbitrators who have decided not to hear certain testimonies or certain witnesses will sometimes go to great lengths in their award, by instinct of self protection, to prevent the losing party from invoking Art. V. 1(b) of the New York Convention (a party "unable to present his case") or another applicable law (English Arbitration Act 1996, sec. 68(2)(d), US Federal Arbitration Act, sec. 10(d)).

26 W. Peter, "Witness 'Conferencing'", Arbitration International, Vol. 18 – No.1 (2002), pp. 47-58.

27 M. Rubino-Sammartano, op. cit., pp. 690-691.

28 G.B. Born, op. cit., p. 93: this was probably not the case ten years ago.

29 Société Ganz Mozdony et autres c/ SNCFT, Paris Court of Appeal, (1st Ch. C), 16 November 1993, Revue de l'arbitrage 1995, No. 3, pp. 477-481.

30 M. Rubino-Sammartano, op. cit., at p. 669.

31 Société Sopip c/ Société El Banco Arabe Espanol et autre, Court of Appeal of Paris (1st Ch. C), 14 December 1999, commented in Revue de l'Arbitrage 2000, No. 3, pp. 471-492, at p. 481.

32 M. Schneider, "Witnesses in International Arbitration", presentation of materials from arbitration practice, ASA Bulletin, No. 2, 1993, 302 at p. 310 and No. 4, 1993, 568 at pp. 575-576.

33 G. B. Born, op. cit., p. 88; Fouchard Gaillard Goldman, op. cit., para. 1287; Y. Derains and E. Schwartz, op. cit., p. 269.

34 A. Redfern and M. Hunter, op. cit., para. 6-105, p. 336.

35 ICC, Taking of Evidence in International Arbitral Proceedings, Paris, 1990; J. Thorens, "L'arbitre international au point de rencontre des traditions du droit civil et de la common law", Etudes de droit international en l'honneur de Pierre Lalive, recueil édité par C. Dominicé, R. Patry et C. Reymond, Helbing & Lichtenhahn. 1993, pp. 693-697; Procedure and the Taking of Evidence in International Commercial Arbitration, The Interaction of Civil Law and Common Law Procedures, P.M. Patocchi & I.L. Meakin, RDAI/IBLJ, No. 7, 1996, pp. 884-895; A.H. Baum, "Reconciling Anglo-Saxon and Civil Law Procedure: The Path to a Procedural Lex Arbitrationis", Law of International Business and Dispute Settlement in the 21st Century: Liber Amicorum Karl-Heinz Böekstiegel, edited by R. Briner, L.Y. Fortier, K.P. Berger & J. Bredow, 2001, p. 21; see also

P. Mayer, op. cit., supra, note 12; H. Smith, Roles of the Arbitral Tribunal in Civil Law and Common Law Systems with Respect to Presentation of Evidence, ICCA Congress Series No. 7, op. cit., supra, note 16, pp. 161-172; J. Paulsson, Overview of Methods of Presenting Evidence in Different Legal Systems, Id., pp. 112-122.

36 See in this connection the guidelines proposed by D.W. Rivkin, "Procedural Issues to Consider", Chapter I, in the Practitioner's Handbook on International Arbitration and Mediation, edited by R.V. Rhoodes, D.M. Kolkey, R. Chernick, Juris Publishing, 2003, at para. 6.06.

37 J.-F. Poudret and S. Besson, op. cit., para. 560, p. 512.

38 R. Best, United Kingdom: High Court Finds Unfairness in Disclosure of Pharmaceutical Company's Dawn Raided Documents, commenting on R v Director of the Serious Fraud Office & Secretary of State for Health (2003) EWHC 3002 (Admin), 17 December 2003, available on www.mondaq.com, 23 January 2004.

39 J.-L. Delvolvé, J. Rouche and G.H. Pointon, French Arbitration Law and Practice, Kluwer Law International, 2003, para. 240, p. 129.

40 M. Bühler and C. Dorgan, op. cit., Section 4E.

3

Practices of the horseshed:

The preparation of witnesses by counsel in America

By Robert S. Rifkind
Senior Counsel, Cravath, Swaine & Moore LLP, USA

International arbitration almost inevitably brings into contact – if not collision – the different styles, habits, customs and practices that counsel and arbitrators of diverse backgrounds bring to proceedings. It is surely the course of wisdom that those differences be made patent rather than be left in the twilight of rumour and anecdote. In that context, I assume, I have been asked to describe, in practical terms, how American lawyers prepare witnesses to testify.

Although the literature on this subject is neither extensive nor markedly analytic, the practices I shall describe are long-standing and well established. That the business of preparing witnesses comes down to us from earlier times is reflected in the fact that it is commonly known as horseshedding[1] – an allusion to the modest structure behind the rural courthouse where once counsel found it convenient to confer with witnesses before calling them to testify.

I recognize that what is normal and expected in the United States is viewed with grave suspicion and, indeed, at least in the realm of judicial proceedings, prohibited in much of Europe[2]. So let me make full disclosure at the outset: in the world in which I have practised law the failure of counsel adequately to prepare the witnesses both for direct and for cross-examination would be regarded as a serious dereliction of professional duty[3].

How it is that two such different approaches have developed is beyond my assignment and my capacity to explain, but I have no doubt that the American practice is to be understood only in the larger context of the style and character of our adversarial approach to the proof of contested facts. It is not too great a simplification to say that an evidentiary hearing in the United States is a specialized type of drama in which opposing parties attempt to present their story to the finder of fact through the questioning and cross-questioning of witnesses. The burden of making that process work – that is, of getting a coherent, credible and persuasive account presented through the questioning of witnesses – falls almost entirely on counsel. Each lawyer is the director of a little play. He must choreograph the entrances and exits of the players and elicit their answers in an order that results in an account of some past events that is coherent, comprehensible, persuasive, and, if possible, interesting to the finder of fact. In such a theatrical production, documents and other tangible evidence may be important, even indispensable, props – like smoking guns or bloodstained daggers – but the organizing narrative is provided by oral testimony. On this stage the lawyer cannot do his job without knowing what the witnesses he calls will say and, so far as possible, what will be said by each of his adversary's witnesses. Likewise, the witnesses cannot do their job without a good idea of what will be asked of them by counsel.

How then does the lawyer proceed? The answer, so far as I am aware, does not depend significantly on the type of tribunal before which the witness is to appear, and I will not distinguish between arbitration and litigation here. The lawyer's conversations with the potential witnesses will begin long before they are identified as witnesses. Counsel for claimant will of necessity have interviewed many of the individuals who may have knowledge bearing on the client's claim even before the first pleading is drafted. Indeed, under our Federal Rules of Civil Procedure, counsel's signature on a pleading constitutes his certification that, to the best of his knowledge, information and belief, "formed after an inquiry reasonable under the circumstances", the claims asserted are not only "warranted" as a matter of law, but are based on factual contentions that have "evidentiary support or, if specifically so identified, are likely to have evidentiary support after a reasonable opportunity for further investigation or discovery"[4]. The violation of that rule is grounds for the imposition of sanctions on counsel, and substantial fines have in fact been imposed.

So counsel will inevitably interview as many people as he can get access to. He will review his client's relevant files and then go back again to the individuals so as to be sure that he understands the strengths and weaknesses of the case. He will talk to non-party witnesses. He will probably not talk to officers or other employees of the adverse party for obvious reasons including the prohibition on communicating directly with someone represented by counsel without the consent of such other lawyer[5].

As this exploratory process proceeds, the lawyer will begin to make judgements as to the utility or inutility of the cast of characters before him. Who knows the key facts? Who can testify to them with the greatest clarity and persuasive effect? Who becomes inarticulate or stutters under stress? Who is untrustworthy or comes across as untrustworthy? Who will be available at the likely time of trial? From all these and other considerations, the lawyer will select his witnesses and then begin the serious work of preparing them to testify.

Four things need to be achieved in this process:

- **First**, the witness must be put at ease and made to feel comfortable with the task at hand.
- **Second**, the witness must be given an understanding of the process in which he is to participate and how his part of the story fits into the overall picture.
- **Third**, the witness must be intimately engaged in a dialogue that results in an outline of the questions and answers that will comprise his direct testimony.
- **Fourth**, the witness must be prepared in detail, so far as humanly possible, for every difficulty that he will face on cross-examination.

Most people approach virtually any public performance with apprehension and the prospect of giving testimony with dread. If the witness is to do an effective job in presenting his evidence to the finder of fact, he must be made to feel that he can cope with the task, that he is in good hands, and that no harm will come to him. The lawyer tries to give the witness every assurance that he will be prepared for the ordeal ahead and that the lawyer will keep him out of trouble.

If it does not already exist, the lawyer will, if possible, establish an attorney-client relationship with the witness, thereby permitting the witness to pour out his heart in confidence to the lawyer and permitting the lawyer to give privileged advice to the witness. Where there is a real potential for divergence in the interests of the witness and the interests of the party calling him (as may be the case, for example, where the witness is a director of a corporation and the lawyer represents the corporate entity), the lawyer may well have an obligation to advise the witness to consult with his own counsel[6] who may wish to attend and participate in the preparatory sessions.

In all events, the witness is told about the physical arrangements of the forum in which he will testify, who the other players in the drama are, and the mechanics of giving testimony. Further, he must be advised that he will be under oath and that false testimony will subject him to the possibility of prosecution for perjury. It can not be emphasized enough that nothing will destroy the witness's confidence in counsel faster, nothing will destroy his utility as a witness more thoroughly, and nothing is more counter-productive than the slightest suggestion to the witness that he is being called upon to give false testimony. Perhaps it is a sign of our cynical times, but some witnesses show up assuming that that is what they are going to be asked to do. They must be disabused of that idea. They must be told that nothing can do more harm to the case. They must be encouraged to believe that the lawyer is capable of coping with any true fact, but that deception will be detected and that being detected will destroy the credibility of the witness and very likely the cause.

Having established the appropriate environment for serious discussion, the lawyer will want to be sure the witness has a good idea of the nature of the case and how his testimony fits into the larger picture. It is often appropriate to give the witness a copy of the pleadings, or the terms of reference, or some early decision by the tribunal, any of which may serve, in an even-handed way, to identify the issues. It is not useful to give the witness a highly one-sided account, either orally or in writing, of the controversy. The witness really needs to understand what both sides are saying and what is, therefore, in dispute. Further, the witness may well be cross-examined about whatever documents were shown him[7] and, if all he saw was a highly partisan account, it will not enhance his credibility with the finder of fact.

Having established the big picture, the lawyer and witness need to walk through the facts that the witness is going to testify about. If his narrative will be helped by documents, he needs to be shown them and asked to read them carefully. If diagrams, pictures, tables or the like are going to be helpful, they must be reviewed by him at this time. If his memory needs to be refreshed, he must review whatever will remind him of something he has forgotten or is uncertain about.

This is a slow process. If the testimony is complicated or lengthy, it is likely to take more than one session. As it goes along, the lawyer is developing his line of questions and the witness is developing facility in responding to them. Collectively, they are identifying the best examples to be used, the points that need to be presented at length, those than can be abbreviated, and those that are too complicated to be worth making. The lawyer may also give advice on order, pace, style and even the choice of words that will make the witness's point particularly clear or avoid ambiguity[8].

This sort of detailed preparation is particularly important insofar as the rules preclude the use of leading questions on direct examination[9]. As one treatise correctly asserts:

> "Thorough preparation of the witness stands as an essential element of avoiding the leading question. Before he takes the stand, the witness should know what each of your questions is aimed at. If you and he have gone over every step of his testimony, questions such as 'what happened next?' 'What if anything did you do then?' will not puzzle him."[10]

It may be suggested that all of this labour of both witness and counsel can be minimized by the use of witness statements in lieu of direct examination. Perhaps it is easier for the lawyer simply to sit down and draft what he hopes the witness will say, have the witness look it over, and then submit it. I think in reality, however, testimony written out in advance, while convenient for the tribunal, requires special pains by counsel and the witness if the witness is going to be able to survive cross-examination. Whether one uses written or oral testimony, I do not believe there is any shortcut for the painful and slow job of working through the witness's testimony with the witness to make sure that the story that is being told is a story that the witness is prepared and willing truthfully to tell.

In this process the expert-witness requires special care. The distinguished professor of medicine or economics cannot address the finder of fact as he would lecture to his graduate students. He has first to teach counsel what counsel needs to know about his field, and then, usually, counsel has to help him present the matter in terms and in an order that can be clearly and quickly understood by the non-expert finder of fact.

Whether expert or factual witnesses are involved, none of this is a matter of memorizing lines. Some witnesses attempt to do that. Maybe some lawyers encourage them to do it. Memorized lines are a recipe for disaster. The script never works out as planned. The tribunal asks you to proceed in some unexpected order or intervenes with some unexpected question and the witness whose only hold on his testimony is a memorized text is lost at sea. Even if the witness survives questioning by the tribunal, the skilled cross-examiner takes the witness back to his prepared lines, and when they come out exactly the same way the second time and perhaps the third time, they look plainly disingenuous.

The world being an imperfect place, it is not unusual for counsel to come across unhelpful facts during the course of this process. Counsel then has to decide whether to bring them out on direct and thereby, hopefully, defuse them, or leave them to his adversary to bring them out on cross, with maximum dramatic effect. There is seldom an easy answer to this problem. It calls for judgement. But if you believe that the credibility of the witness is as important as the substance of his testimony, then you will frequently come to the conclusion that to bring out the harmful fact on direct is the lesser of evils and may have a usefully disarming effect. Conversely, it is usually a mistake to proceed on the assumption that the unhappy fact will not emerge on cross.

Sometimes, of course, you learn during witness preparation something that leads you to change course altogether. You find, for example, that your eminent and expensive expert economist wrote a learned article expressing a view diametrically opposed to what he is now saying. You may well decide that his genial explanation that "that was written a long time ago, and I have grown older and wiser" will not dissuade the finder of fact from concluding that the expert, on whose awesome authority you hoped to rest, is a mere opportunist. In such a case it is usually best to find another expert.

And sometimes you find that a fact witness is mistaken in his recollection of the course of events. He has placed someone at a meeting who could not have been there. Or omitted from the meeting someone who was there. He has gotten the sequence of events jumbled. He has assumed that something was done that didn't get done. Here the lawyer must do the best he can to help get the witness straightened out. He must show the witness the relevant minutes or correspondence or whatever else may help. Of course, the witness can only testify on the basis of his own knowledge and memory, but the lawyer should do his best to test the accuracy of that memory and forestall demonstrably mistaken testimony. If the lawyer fails to help, he leaves the witness needlessly exposed to damaging cross-examination, or even charges of perjury, and, not least, he himself may violate the rules of professional ethics under which a lawyer may not knowingly "offer evidence that the lawyer knows to be false."[11]

When the scope, substance and style of direct examination have been worked out, attention turns to the preparation for cross-examination. The principle object of cross-examination is to damage the witness's credibility, to show that he is biased, has faulty memory, is given to exaggeration, is ignorant of what he claims to know, or that he knows facts or has made statements inconsistent with his direct testimony. Notwithstanding the witness-stand confessions that are the standard fare of courtroom dramas on television, in real life it is rare that a witness can be brought to repudiate his direct testimony altogether. But damage to credibility is not so rare and can be very serious. As I have indicated, the witness's credibility may be as important as – or perhaps more important than – the substance of his testimony. Consciously or unconsciously, the finder of fact is very likely to draw a negative inference not only about the witness who has been shown to be untrustworthy, but also about the lawyer who called him in the first place and about the party on whose behalf he was called. This consideration will have heavily influenced the preparation for direct examination, but it requires special attention and care in the preparation for cross.

There is a long litany of things that one normally tells a witness at this point. He must be told to listen carefully to the question asked, be sure he understands it, and have it repeated or explained if he doesn't understand it. His answer must be based on his own knowledge and his own memory. If his memory is uncertain, he should indicate his degree of uncertainty. His answer must not be based on speculation, guesses, or assumptions. Unless he is an expert-witness, he should not answer hypothetical questions or offer his opinions. He is entitled to explain his answer. He need not be confined to a yes or no. He should, as a rule, only respond to the question put and not volunteer what has not been asked for.

All this is a little like giving someone a manual on how to ride a bicycle. It is no substitute for practical experience. The critical element of preparing a witness is to stage a moot cross-examination, making it as realistic as possible. Ideally, the lawyer in charge of the direct examination will ask another lawyer to prepare and conduct a very thorough moot cross-examination. Having another lawyer do this adds to the realism of the exercise, leaves lead counsel free to play the role he will play at the evidentiary hearing, and helps lead counsel preserve a cordial relationship with the witness notwithstanding the roughness with which the moot cross-examination may be conducted. Most important, this leaves lead counsel free to watch how his witness bears up under cross and free to interject advice when he sees difficulty.

If this process is carried out with real thoroughness, one hopes the witness will have been confronted with every possible difficulty he should experience at the hearing. He will have been confronted with every document with which his testimony may be challenged. Every prior statement that could be thought to be inconsistent with his testimony will be thrown at him. Potential problems that could be forestalled by appropriate inquiry during direct will be folded into the plan for direct examination. Ideally, the witness will be immunized against surprise at the hearing. He will also, if necessary, become more circumspect in answering questions. He will have learned the dangers of exaggeration, of inappropriate enthusiasm or untimely jest. If all goes well, after the hearing the witness will tell you that the moot cross-examination was vastly more challenging than the real thing.

Some lawyers have taken to videotaping the moot cross and then replaying all or parts of it so that the witness can see for himself how he looks and sounds. I do not do this because I think it deflects attention from a sharp focus on the questions and answers and because it tends to make witnesses more nervous and self-conscious. The witness must emerge from preparation with a realistic sense of self-confidence and a sense that he can cope with the ordeal ahead.

As one concludes this long journey with the witness one will say a few words about where and when he is to appear, what if anything he is to bring with him, the need for a good night's sleep beforehand, what to wear and so on.

I have no doubt that the process I have been describing can be abused. I suppose there are lawyers willing to foreswear their professional obligations and to advise witnesses to give false testimony, or subtlety prompt them to do so, or wink at what they know to be false. The lawyer who does so violates the undertakings he gave when he was admitted to his profession and very likely does grave harm to his client into the bargain. In all events, the potential for abuse is not unique to this aspect of the lawyer's work. Lawyers have, on occasion, been found to suppress documents they were called upon to produce or, indeed, to alter or forge documents to be offered in evidence. Lawyers have been known to embezzle clients' funds. But then too, I suppose there may be corrupt finders of fact or, more likely, lazy or biased finders of fact. At least when it comes to the preparation of witnesses, the threat of exposure by skilful cross-examination stands as a great deterrent to falsification.

Of this I am sure: In a system that regards the oral examination of witnesses as central to the process of finding disputed facts, the preparation of witnesses for their vital role is not only indispensable but results in a vast increase in the truth-content of the testimony and greatly facilitates the work of the fact-finder.

END NOTES

1 "Horseshedding" is defined as "the instruction of a witness favorable to one's case (esp. a client) about the proper method of responding to questions while giving testimony". Blacks Law Dictionary (7th ed. 1999).

2 See Hans van Houtte, "Counsel-Witness Relations and Professional Misconduct in Civil Law Systems", Arbitration International, Vol. 14, No. 4 (2003).

3 American Law Institute, Restatement of the Law: The Law Governing Lawyers (2000), § 116(1) and Comment (a) and (b).

"Under litigation practice, uniformly followed in the United States, a lawyer might interview prospective witnesses prior to their testifying. . . As a practical matter, rules requiring inquiry to support factual allegations in a complaint or other document. . . may require a lawyer to interview witnesses to gain the necessary factual foundation. Competent preparation for trial. . . might also require pre-testimonial interviews with witnesses." Id. at Comment (b).

4 Federal Rules of Civil Procedure, Rule 11(b).

5 See, e.g., New York Code of Professional Responsibility, DR 7-104.

6 See, e.g., New York Code of Professional Responsibility, DR 5-107B, DR 5-109.

7 See, e.g., Federal Rules of Evidence, Rule 612.

8 See, American Law Institute, Restatement of the Law: The Law Governing Lawyers §116, Comment b.

9 See, e.g., Federal Rules of Evidence, Rule 611(c).

10 Walter Barthold, "Direct and Cross-examination", in Federal Civil Practice (G.M. Vairo, ed.) (N.Y.S. Bar Association, 1989), pp. 644-45.

11 ABA Model Rules of Professional Conduct, Rule 3.3(a)(4).

4

Witness statements

By Anne Véronique Schlaepfer
Partner, Schellenberg Wittmer, Switzerland

INTRODUCTION

Consistent with the common law practice of affidavits and the practice of "*déclarations de tiers*" before some civil law courts[1], arbitration rules often provide that witness testimony may be contained in a statement in writing.

In fact, the production of witness statements has become common practice in international arbitration[2].

Usually, the parties submit witness statements with (or sometimes after) their memorials. Then, in the course of the evidentiary hearings, the witnesses orally confirm their statement and may be cross-examined by the opposing party (and re-examined if the party which submitted the witness statement so wishes).

The advantages of this practice are the following:

- It enables the parties to narrow the issues to be addressed at the evidentiary hearing.
- It assists the parties and the arbitral tribunal to prepare for the evidentiary hearing.
- It assists the arbitral tribunal to determine whether a specific witness testimony is relevant to the dispute (if it is not, the principle of efficiency would suggest that the witness should not be summoned to appear at the hearing), or whether it is sufficiently well-informed through other evidence and does not need to hear the witness. Indeed, arbitrators may decide, given the specific circumstances of the case, not to hear witnesses or all the witnesses a party wishes to examine[3] (see "The Confirmation of the Witness Statement", page 70). For example, Article 20.3 of the ICC Rules

of Arbitration provides that the arbitral tribunal *"may decide to hear witnesses* (…)"; similarly, Article 20.2 of the LCIA Arbitration Rules provides that the arbitral tribunal *"has a discretion to allow, refuse, or limit the appearance of witnesses (whether of fact or expert-witness)"*.

- As a result, it increases the efficiency of the proceedings by reducing the length of the evidentiary hearings.

Even if witness statements are generally accepted in international arbitration, experience shows that parties, counsel and arbitrators not always agree on their purpose, their content and the way they should be used in the proceedings.

Although there is no codification of arbitration procedure, arbitration practitioners may refer to different sources in order to clarify misunderstandings and avoid unjustified expectations. In particular, the 1999 IBA Rules on the Taking of Evidence (the IBA Rules)[4], which are meant to reflect the current practice in international arbitration, constitute a useful tool. However, they do not directly apply, unless the parties have adopted them. In practice, it appears that parties and arbitral tribunals often use them as guidelines in developing their own procedures. Parties and arbitral tribunals may, of course, choose a procedural arrangement that differs from the ones suggested by the IBA Rules.

Some arbitral institutions have adopted specific provisions regarding witness evidence[5]. Moreover, the procedural rules regarding the taking of evidence drafted by arbitral tribunals also often contain useful information.

Given their importance in practice, I will address below some of the issues that arise in the context of the preparation and confirmation (or lack thereof) of witness statements.

Then, in conclusion, I will briefly discuss the efficiency of witness statements. To what extent do arbitral tribunals take witness statements into consideration when deliberating and drafting the award?

THE PREPARATION OF WITNESS STATEMENTS

1. When should it take place?

From counsel's point of view, it should take place as soon as possible, namely, as soon as one knows the issues at stake and the facts to be proven. Indeed, it allows the parties (and counsel):

- To determine which witnesses they may rely upon and what kind of information they are in a position to provide.
- To prevent, at least to a large extent, the opposing party from obtaining witness statements from "their" own witnesses (former employees, consultants, etc.).
- To ensure that the witnesses will be available at some point in time to work on their statement.

2. What information should witness statements contain?

According to Article 4.5 of the IBA Rules, witness statements shall contain:

> "(a) The full name and address of the witness, his or her present and past relationship (if any) with any of the Parties, and a description of his or her background, qualifications, training and experience, if such a description may be relevant and material to the dispute or to the contents of the statement;
>
> (b) a full and detailed description of the facts, and the source of the witness's information as to those facts, sufficient to serve as that witness's evidence in the matter in dispute;
>
> (c) an affirmation of the truth of the statement; and
>
> (d) the signature of the witness and its date and place."

Some arbitrators specify that a picture of the witness shall be provided with the statement.

Witness statements do not constitute an additional opportunity for the parties to submit new factual allegations or to modify their prayers for relief, even if the witness statement is signed by a party representative. Factual allegations and prayers for relief must be contained in the memorials submitted by the parties. Witness statements are a means of adducing evidence, incomplete to the extent that they have to be confirmed orally at the hearing (unless the parties agree or the arbitral tribunal decides otherwise) (see "The Confirmation of the Witness Statement", page 70), and should be treated as such by arbitral tribunals, irrespective of their actual content.

In practice, the submission of additional memorials entitled "witness statement" often proves to be useless, if not completely counter-productive.

3. Is it possible to attach documents to witness statements?

In principle, unless the parties or the arbitral tribunal decide otherwise, nothing prevents witnesses from attaching documents to their statements, to the extent that these documents relate to the content of their testimony. For example, a witness explaining that he personally supervised specific marketing studies (which the opposing party disputes) may wish to annex to his statement the facsimiles and e-mails that he sent in this context.

However, the submission of witness statements should not become a convenient way for the parties to produce documents they were not in a position or forgot to produce in a timely manner. In order to prevent the development of such a practice, documents attached to a witness statement should be viewed as a part of this statement and evaluated as such by the arbitral tribunal. To avoid any misunderstanding, if a party intends to rely on a document provided by a witness, for example to prove other factual allegations contained in its written submissions, it should produce the document as an exhibit, if the applicable procedural rules permit it at this stage of the proceedings.

If specific documents are cited in the witness statement without being attached to it, the opposing party should be entitled to obtain the production of these documents. However, a request to produce all the documents that the witness may have used to prepare his statement would be excessive.

4. What should be the role of counsel?

It is now generally accepted in international arbitration that counsel may have contact with witnesses prior to the evidentiary hearings[6]. However, if it appears in a given case that parties and counsel are not experienced in international arbitration and / or come from different legal traditions (in some legal systems preparing witnesses may be contrary to lawyers' ethical rules), the arbitral tribunal should ensure that the same rules regarding the preparation of witnesses apply to all parties[7].

It is also accepted that witnesses usually do not write their statements themselves. The practice of having the last page of the statement only containing the date and the signature of the witness (in different characters from the other pages of the document) does not seem to surprise anyone anymore.

In practice, counsel often helps the witness to focus on the relevant issues. He then reviews the statement or drafts it on the basis of the story told by the witness, who should approve the text. This way of proceeding usually facilitates the submission of witness statements, which the opposing party and the arbitral tribunal may understand.

However, counsel would be well advised to use the witness' own words and expressions, as long as they are understandable. This would make the witness statement more credible (and often more interesting). Moreover, the impact on the arbitral tribunal may be rather negative, if it appears at the evidentiary hearing that the witness does not understand the words used in his own statement (see "The Impact of Witness Statements on the Result of the Arbitration", page 73).

In any event, the story has, of course, to be that of the witness, not the product of the party's (or counsel's) imagination or wishes[8].

THE SUBMISSION OF WITNESS STATEMENTS

One of the issues frequently discussed in the course of procedural hearings relates to the timing of the submission of the witness statements. Should they be filed with the memorials or afterwards?

The answer obviously depends on the circumstances of each arbitral proceeding. However, parties may be less tempted to view witness statements as additional memorials and to submit bundles of documents attached to them if the witness statements and the memorials have to be filed simultaneously.

THE CONFIRMATION OF THE WITNESS STATEMENT

First, it may be useful to emphasise that the arbitral tribunal can decide that the witness statements, or some of them, will not be confirmed orally[9]. Indeed, as stated by the Swiss Federal Tribunal in a recent decision dated January 7, 2004, arbitrators may consider that, given the circumstances of the case, it is not justified to summon witnesses who submitted witness statements to appear at an evidentiary hearing. Such a decision does not imply, however, that the arbitral tribunal will not take these witness statements into consideration when weighing the evidence produced by the parties[10].

Assuming that the arbitral tribunal does not make such a decision (which should not occur very often, since the tendency in international arbitration is not to take into account witness statements which have not been confirmed orally or are not corroborated by other evidence), one may refer to the approach adopted in the IBA Rules. Indeed, procedural orders rendered by arbitral tribunals regarding the taking of evidence often contain similar rules. Since this approach seems to be the most frequent one in practice, it is useful to address some of the difficulties that it may cause.

Pursuant to Article 4.7 of the IBA Rules:

> "Each witness who has submitted a Witness Statement shall appear for testimony at an evidentiary hearing, unless the Parties agree otherwise".

Parties and arbitrators may face the following situations:

■ The usual case

One party wishes to cross-examine a witness presented by the opposite party. The witness is summoned and appears at the evidentiary hearing. His oral testimony (during the examination in chief and/or cross-examination) confirms the content of his witness statement. The witness statement and the testimony together constitute evidence. When making its decision, the arbitral tribunal will evaluate them.

■ The witness does not appear at the hearing

The witness is summoned to the hearing, but fails to appear, without giving any reason. According to Article 4.8 of the IBA Rules:

> "If a witness who has submitted a Witness Statement does not appear without a valid reason for testimony at an evidentiary hearing, except by agreement of the Parties, the Arbitral Tribunal shall disregard that Witness Statement unless, in exceptional circumstances, the Arbitral Tribunal determines otherwise".

Thus, unless the witness gives a valid reason or the parties agree not to hear the witness, the witness statement shall be disregarded. The arbitral tribunal may decide otherwise in exceptional circumstances, such as the death of the witness. In this event, it will take into consideration the witness statement, notwithstanding the witness's failure to appear at the evidentiary hearing.

- **There is an agreement of the parties not to hear the witness**

The parties agree that there is no need to hear the witness. According to Article 4.9 of the IBA Rules:

> "If the Parties agree that a witness who has submitted a Witness Statement does not need to appear for testimony at an evidentiary hearing, such an agreement shall not be considered to reflect an agreement as to the correctness of the content of Witness Statement".

In this event, the arbitral tribunal should not disregard the witness statement. It has to evaluate it notwithstanding the lack of oral confirmation (which may prove difficult, given that the arbitral tribunal is not in a position to ascertain the credibility of the witness).

- **The opposing party does not intend to cross-examine the witness**

The opposing party does not intend to cross-examine the witness. In this event, may the arbitral tribunal or the other party require that the witness appear to give testimony?

As far as the arbitral tribunal is concerned, there is little doubt that it can decide to summon the witness if it deems appropriate.

According to the IBA Rules (see Article 4.9 *a contrario*), the party submitting the witness statement may also request the appearance of the witness. Nonetheless, in practice, witness statements are often meant to replace direct examination[11]. As a result, arbitral tribunals sometimes consider that only the party wishing to cross-examine the witness may request the appearance of the witness. This position is not satisfactory for the following reasons:

First, it means that the party submitting the witness statement has no control whatsoever over the appearance of its own witnesses at the evidentiary hearing (which could prevent the witness from confirming his statement).

Second, if arbitral tribunals come to the conclusion that witness statements replace direct examination, they should also consider them as such when deciding the case, even if no cross-examination has taken place. I very much doubt that this is actually the case, especially when, at the same time, some arbitral tribunals do not view witness statements as such as evidence, if the witness has not been heard. Moreover, the tendency in international arbitration is to give little credence to witness statements, especially when the witness is not heard in the course of an evidentiary hearing (see "The Impact of Witness Statements on the Result of the Arbitration", page 73).

As a result, the best solution is certainly to authorize both parties to request the appearance of witnesses, even if the parties have agreed or the arbitral tribunal has ordered that witness statements shall serve as the witness's direct testimony. In this case, according to the principle of efficiency of the arbitral proceedings, direct examination may be limited to a confirmation by the witness of the accuracy of his statement with, perhaps, some additional (limited) explanations of some major issues.

In any event, arbitral tribunals should clarify at the beginning of the proceedings whether written statements will be treated as direct testimony. Arbitral tribunals should also make certain that all parties understand the consequences of such a decision.

THE CONTENT OF THE ORAL TESTIMONY

In principle, the scope of direct examination (if there is any) should be limited by the content of the witness statement (unless new issues have arisen since the submission of the statement, or the parties agree otherwise). Otherwise, the submission of such a statement would prove pointless. In fact, direct examination should normally be limited to confirming or explaining in a more detailed manner major issues addressed in the statement (without repeating the content of the statement). Sometimes, it may be sufficient to have the witness merely confirm that the content of the statement is accurate.

Obviously the scope of cross-examination cannot be limited in the same way. Otherwise, a party could prevent the opposing party from asking relevant questions by submitting witness statements dealing with side issues only.

THE IMPACT OF WITNESS STATEMENTS ON THE RESULT OF THE ARBITRATION

One often wonders to what extent arbitral tribunals take into account witness statements when making their decision. Obviously, there is no one answer to this question. Each arbitrator may have a different approach. However, there seems to be a trend not to take witness statements into account, unless the witness gives convincing explanations during the evidentiary hearing or other reliable evidence corroborates them.

Such a result is not surprising. Indeed, since it is widely accepted that witness statements are not written by the witness himself, the only way to ascertain whether the wording of the statement genuinely reflects the message that the witness intended to convey is to hear this witness[12]. Hence, it is understandable that arbitral tribunals are reluctant to refer in their awards to witness statements, which have not been orally confirmed.

In conclusion, it seems that witness statements give rise to contradictory tendencies. There is no doubt that they are widely used in international arbitration. Frequently, they are meant to serve as direct testimony, notwithstanding the fact that they do not look like written statements made by witnesses. At the same time, arbitrators seem to be increasingly reluctant to take them into account as such, unless the credibility of the witness has been tested during the evidentiary hearing or other reliable evidence confirms the accuracy of the statement. In other words, witness statements are supposed to increase the efficiency of the arbitral proceedings but seem to be a rather ineffective means to convince arbitral tribunals.

As a result, counsel and parties would be well advised to make certain that witness statements do not look like lawyers' briefs and that witnesses who submit written statements are given an opportunity to appear at the evidentiary hearings.

END NOTES

1 See articles 199ss of the Nouveau Code de Procédure Civile.

2 Laurent Lévy, "Witness Statements", in De Lege Ferenda, Etudes pour le professeur Alain Hirsch, 2004, p. 96; Paolo Michele Patocchi and Ian Meakin, "Procedure and The Taking of Evidence in International Commercial Arbitration", The Interaction of Civil Law and Common Law Procedures, RDAI/IBLJ, No. 7, 1996; Derains/Schwartz, A Guide to the New ICC Rules of Arbitration, 1998, p. 257; Redfern/Hunter, Law and Practice of International Commercial Arbitration, third edition, 1999, par. 6-78.

3 Fouchard/Gaillard/Goldmann, On International Commercial Arbitration, 1999, par. 1277; Redfern/Hunter, Law and Practice of International Commercial Arbitration, third edition, 1999, par. 6-78; Poudret/Besson, Droit comparé de l'arbitrage international, 2002, par. 553; Lew/Mistelis/Kröll, Comparative International Commercial Arbitration, 2003, par. 22-69; Decision of the Swiss Federal Tribunal published in ATF 119 II 386; Decision of the Court of Appeal in Dalmia Dairy Industries Ltd (1978) 2 Lloyd's Rep. 223, 270: the sole arbitrator sitting in London refused to hear certain witnesses. In the context of a subsequent enforcement action, the Court of Appeal stated that, according to the then applicable Article 20 of the ICC Rules, the arbitrator had a discretion but not an obligation to hear witnesses.

4 IBA Rules on the Taking of Evidence in International Commercial Arbitration, 1 June 1999.

5 See for example the LCIA Rules, 1 January 1998, Article 20.

6 Georg von Segesser, "Witness Preparation in International Commercial Arbitration", Swiss Arbitration Association (ASA) Bulletin, No. 2, 2002, p. 224; David Roney, Effective Witness Preparation For International Commercial Arbitration: A Practical Guide For Counsel in Journal of International Arbitration 2003, 20(5), p. 429ss.

7 Fouchard/Gaillard/Goldmann, On International Commercial Arbitration, 1999, par. 1285.

8 Even if in some States, notably in Switzerland, the submission of a witness statement containing inaccurate information would probably not constitute a criminal offence, the actual impact of such a document on the party's case may be disastrous.

9 Karl-Heinz Böckstiegel, "Experience as an Arbitrator Using the UNCITRAL Arbitration Rules", in Etudes de droit international en l'honneur de Pierre Lalive, Bâle, 1993, p. 435.

10 In the United States, see the Decision rendered by the United States District Court, Southern District of New York on 12 January 1993, Arbitration Between Intercarbon Bermuda Ltd. vs Caltex Trading and Transport Corp., published in XIX Y. B. COM. ARB.802 (1994): "The Court is mindful of the factors weighing against the arbitrator's decision to render judgment on the documentary evidence alone: the importance of hearings to most arbitration proceedings; the weakness of affidavits as bases for summary determinations; and the repeated desire of InterCarbon to present live testimony. Despite these considerations, the arbitrator's decision is reasonable and does not amount to misconduct. Hearings will not be required just to see whether real issues surface (....)." One may assume that the opinion recently expressed by the United States Supreme Court in a criminal case, according to which the defendant's constitutional right of confrontation and cross-examination is violated if an eyewitness is not available at trial (because of marital privilege) would not apply in the context of international arbitration (Crawford vs Washington, March 8, 2004).

11 See Article 8.3 of the IBA Rules; Michael Bühler, Carroll Dorgan, "Witness Testimony Pursuant to the 1999 IBA Rules of Evidence in International Commercial Arbitration" in Journal of International Arbitration 17(1): 3-30, 2000.

12 "The practice of taking factual witness statements requires urgent reform. Increasingly, many international arbitrators pay little credence to written witness statements on any contentious issue, unless independently corroborated by other reliable evidence. It is perhaps surprising that many sophisticated practitioners have not yet understood that their massive efforts at re-shaping the testimony of their client's factual witnesses is not only ineffective but often counter-productive." (V.V. Veeder, the 2001 Goff Lecture, "The Lawyer's Duty to Arbitrate in Good Faith, Arbitration International, 2002, Vol. 18, No. 4, p. 445)".

5

Oral evidence and experts in arbitration

By David Brown
Partner, Shadbolt & Co., France
Council Member, ICC Institute of World Business Law

INTRODUCTION

The procedural stage of the international commercial arbitration process is generally characterised by a high degree of flexibility. And flexibility is particularly necessary when dealing with the issue of witness evidence, since parties to arbitration proceedings are liable to come from countries having legal cultures with fundamentally different conceptions as to the role of witnesses. The differences are likely to be even more marked when it comes to the role of experts in legal proceedings, as will be discussed below.

One of the successes of the international commercial arbitration process has been that the potential difficulties to which such marked differences in expectations may give rise have largely been avoided. Arbitration laws and, to a greater extent, rules for arbitration proceedings have a part to play here. But these commonly provide no more than a broad framework. It is the custom and practice developed by arbitrators and counsel within this framework that has proved to be the basis for the success of the process, not least as regards the question of evidence from experts.

This brief paper seeks to show why such potential difficulties could arise, by reference to the role of the expert in two still fundamentally different systems, i.e. in French and English civil procedure. It will then discuss the impact of arbitration law and rules, with a view to showing how they generally provided a framework, in more or less general terms, within which a compromise approach to expert evidence has been able to flourish.

EXPERTS IN FRENCH PROCEDURE

French civil procedure typifies the approach adopted in numerous "civil law" jurisdictions, in that it reflects what would appear to someone from a common law jurisdiction as a distrust of oral evidence. The French view was summed up by Antoine Loysel in his "Institutes of Customary Law" first published in the 16th Century:

> *"Qui mieux abreuve, mieux preuve" (a witness who is well wined and dined will testify well).*

This leads to a procedural system in which weight is given primarily to documentary evidence. There has been no real move to promote a greater role for oral evidence on grounds, for example, that direct evidence of a witness could be tested by some form of the cross-examination procedure dear to common law practitioners.

This is not to say that individuals who saw, heard or did something will never be asked to give evidence. Thus, there is an *"enquête"* procedure that allows magistrates to question such individuals directly. And there is the *"expertise"* procedure which is geared to dealing with complex technical issues in particular. This is where the expert plays a central role, although not as a *"witness"* in the common law sense of the term. If anything, experts in French civil proceedings are more on the court's side of the fence.

Thus, in French proceedings, an expert is a court appointee, although generally as a result of an application by a party rather than the *"ex officio"* exercise by the court of its own powers. The expert must be chosen from a court list – in other words, one can only act in French proceedings as an expert if one has been formally recognised as an expert by the State.

Generally only one expert will be appointed. It may be possible to have additional experts appointed but the view is that, in general, one should suffice for any given technical issue, since, in his capacity as an *"auxiliaire de justice"*, the expert is expected to be independent and to act impartially. Finally, the expert is paid directly by the court out of costs advances payable by the parties.

The duty of the expert is to report to the court upon the technical issue with which the court requires his assistance. In order to do so it is the expert's further duty to organise the *"expertise"* procedure so that the relevant information can be made available to him. Here, the parties play an important although secondary role. They are likely to be the source of much of the information and documentation that the expert will need, but it is the expert himself who will make the final decision in this regard. And if he requires further information, then the expert is empowered to request it from the parties. He may even question the parties or their representatives himself as to their involvement in matters relating to the issue in question.

The expert will invite the parties to attend site visits or on other occasions when he is gathering information. The purpose here is to give the parties an opportunity to verify that the principle of due process is being repeated by the expert.

Parties must always be allowed an opportunity to make representations to an expert, and these may include *"dires"*, i.e. written representations, which an expert must address in his report. It would, however, be going too far to say that there can or will be a real "question and answer" session during which the parties can assess, for example, the value of the line of enquiry being followed by the expert.

Instead, the parties will have to wait until the expert has rendered his report, upon which they will be free to comment at the hearing at which submissions can be made upon its contents. Experts are occasionally summoned by the court to attend a hearing in order to answer questions from the court. And there may be some opportunity for the parties to put questions, but this can hardly be said to correspond to an opportunity to "examine" the expert as a common law practitioner would understand the term.

Thus, while the court may not be bound by an expert's opinion, the nature of the process is such that the expert is heavily relied upon by the court for assistance on technical issues, and it may be difficult for a party to persuade the court that the expert is wrong.

In conclusion, it is possible to characterise the *"expertise"* procedure as a form of *"mini-trial"*, in which the expert assumes the role of the judge, and it is the parties' task to persuade the expert of their respective positions, given the likelihood that the court will rely upon the Expert's own findings when drawing up their judgement.

EXPERTS IN ENGLISH PROCEDURE

It is fair to say that, traditionally, the role of the expert in English procedure was diametrically opposed to that across the Channel. The English Courts have had power to appoint their own experts for centuries, but have only rarely exercised it. Instead, the expert takes part in civil procedure as an expert-witness chosen by a party to give evidence, including the rendering of an opinion, on technical or otherwise complex matters of relevance to the party's case.

There are no official lists from which experts are chosen. Instead, an expert is expected to be competent to express a view on the issue in question. The expert's competence is likely to be tested by cross-examination, but it is only when drawing up its judgement that the court will actually decide if the witness can be considered to have the necessary expertise.

In practice, an expert appointed by a party will assist the party primarily like any other professional advisor. If, however, the expert is also to assist as a witness in proceedings, then any written report he issued for the purposes of those proceedings must be an impartial product – in other words, the expert must not act as a party advocate.

The common law system replies upon cross-examination to verify whether the expert has acted impartially. Cross-examination has long been considered vital to expose errors and/or bias. Lengthy, probing cross-examination is generally considered to be particularly justified where there are expert witnesses, given the greater likelihood of an expert-witness misleading the court than a witness of fact. And it should be appreciated that there is a long-standing English view that any failure to cross-examine a witness on part of his evidence may be treated by the court as acceptance by the party in question of such evidence.

The role and use of expert witnesses in English proceedings have been substantially updated by the new Civil Procedure Rules and Commercial Court Guide brought out in recent years. The cost and delay resulting from the use of numerous experts had been a concern for some time. One of the steps taken to deal with this problem has been the introduction of the concept of a *"single joint expert"*, which has been acknowledged as having been inspired by the French procedures approach. And the special status of such an expert has been recognised in a recent case[1] where the court held that cross-examination of such an expert must be carried out with restraint.

However, even though there are signs that the traditional dichotomy between the French and English approach is being eroded, there is no fundamental change as yet, particularly as regards the vital role of cross-examination as a means of testing expert evidence.

EXPERTS IN ARBITRATION

The contrasting approaches summarised above reflect rules and practice as they have been developed within distinct legal traditions by local legislators and practitioners, and which will be applied regardless of the origin of parties to the State court proceedings in question.

No such constraints apply, however, when it comes to international arbitration proceedings in England or France, whether they are subject to a particular set of arbitration rules or otherwise. And this broad degree of freedom is to be found generally in jurisdictions having the benefit of modern arbitration legislation, and where modern arbitration rules are applied.

WHAT ARBITRATION LAWS SAY

In modern arbitration legislation, the rules and practice surrounding expert evidence are generally left to be fixed by the arbitrators and/or the parties. This may be by express provision, as is the case under English law[2], or impliedly, as under French law[3].

Thus, the power of the arbitrators and/or parties are similar under French and English law, and the legislation differs mainly insofar as it reflects the English legislator's concern to provide the parties and arbitrators with a detailed check-list as to procedural and evidential matters to be decided, including the question of expert evidence and how the procedure applies to the taking of such evidence.

WHAT ARBITRATION RULES SAY

Comparison of frequently used sets of rules governing international arbitration procedure leads one to the conclusion that while the provisions in relation to procedural and evidentiary matters in general, including expert evidence, are set down in greater detail than in arbitration legislation, there is still a very broad degree of discretion for the parties and arbitrators to organise such matters as they wish. This includes the possibility of having both expert witnesses and tribunal-appointed experts.

Thus, for example, the ICC Arbitration Rules provide at Article 20 for both types of expert, although they only provide expressly for interrogation of tribunal experts by the parties[4]. This is certainly not intended to be taken as a prohibition on the questioning of expert witnesses by the parties.

Two observations require to be made here: firstly, it is only in the latest (i.e. 1998) edition of the ICC Rules that specific reference is made for the first time to expert witnesses, i.e. *"experts appointed by the parties"*[5]. This reference to a common law concept is further evidence of a conscious move to render the ICC Rules, which were originally strongly influenced by civil law rules and practices, truly international.

Secondly, the practice in relation to expert evidence in ICC cases has for many years included recourse to both expert witnesses and tribunal-appointed experts. The ICC Rules have always sought to be, and remain, a broad framework within which the arbitrators and parties have flexibility to decide on the type of expertise they wish.

Strictly speaking, therefore, as regards expert evidence and other evidentiary and procedural matters, the ICC "Rules" are in many instances more a set of principles than detailed rules governing procedure.

Like the ICC Rules, the LCIA Rules also demonstrate a desire to provide a truly international framework for arbitration proceedings. It is submitted, however, that the detailed provisions relating, *inter alia*, to expert evidence at Articles 20 and 21 of the LCIA Rules seem, like the English Arbitration Act 1996, to betray a common law drafting concern to cover all major concerns in relation to the taking of evidence, and can be taken as checklists for the options available to the arbitrators and parties.

A similar concern for detail is to be found in the WIPO Rules at Articles 54 and 55. Once again the arbitrators and parties are effectively provided with guidelines and options for consideration when organising the taking of evidence, whether from expert witnesses or tribunal-appointed experts.

However, not all recent sets of rules regulate in as much detail the issue of expert evidence, and the failure of certain sets of rules to clarify whether there is a role for party experts/expert witnesses as well as for tribunal-appointed witnesses (see for example the CIETAC Rules, the UNCITRAL Rules and the

Rules of the European Court of Arbitration) means that as a matter of prudence the arbitrators (preferably acting in conjunction with the parties) should themselves clarify their position in the event that such evidence is proposed, as well as fixing the procedure that will apply.

If any general conclusions are to be drawn from a comparison of arbitration rules on the question of expert evidence, it is that they avoid regulating in great detail what the oral stage of the process of taking evidence may involve, and in particular whether and, if so, at what stage, a written report or statement of an expert-witness is to be submitted prior to the hearing.

These questions are liable to have a bearing on the question of whether the arbitral proceeding satisfies the requirement of due process, and must be borne in mind by the arbitrators, in particular when organising the proceedings. And if parties or their counsel come from jurisdictions as different as the English and French on the question of expert evidence, and possibly also on other major questions concerning witness and documentary evidence, then it is helpful if arbitrators can draw on rules or guidelines that will help them to address the potentially significant differences in expectations as to expert evidence and other procedural matters that may separate the parties.

Some assistance is provided by the UNCITRAL Notes on Organising Arbitral Proceedings 1996. Thus sections 69 to 73 address in detail the steps to be taken in organising evidence from tribunal-appointed experts in particular. As the title of the UNCITRAL initiative indicates, the notes focus upon practical concerns and are not intended to deal with issues such as the type and scope of questions that may be put during the interrogation of experts, or the weight to be attached by the arbitrators to the evidence that is presented.

Perhaps the most helpful initiative in recent years has been the IBA Rules on the Taking of Evidence in International Commercial Arbitrations published by the International Bar Association in 1999. As the Preamble to the Rules states, they are intended to supplement other rules to be applied in the proceedings and can be adapted to the circumstances of any particular proceeding. However, the underlying principle that those using the Rules are invited to follow is that *"the taking of evidence shall be conducted on the principle that each Party shall be entitled to know, reasonably in advance of any evidentiary hearing, the evidence on which the other Parties rely"*.

The Rules provide for both party-appointed experts (Article 5) and tribunal-appointed experts (Article 6). Detailed provisions effectively summarise the parties' expectations in relation to experts in common law and civil law systems respectively. The provisions in Articles 5 and 6 as to the requirements and procedures to be applied are clearly aimed at allowing parties from a legal system that may not recognise or use one of the two types of experts identified to have a reasonably clear idea of what to expect if the IBA Rule in question is adopted without substantial modification. Indeed, as the Preamble states, the Rules are *"intended to govern ... the taking of evidence in international commercial arbitration, particularly those between Parties from different legal traditions"*.

For both types of expert, the aim, in accordance with the principle enunciated in the Preamble as set out above, is to ensure that the parties have sufficient time to study an expert's report in order to prepare questions for the evidentiary hearing.

The Rules also set out in detail who may question whom, and cover the possibility of a tribunal-appointed expert being questioned not only by the parties but even by a party-appointed expert.

Given that the Rules seek to avoid surprises in direct evidence from witnesses of fact and expert witnesses by their emphasis on the production of written statements/reports setting out the evidence in advance of the hearing, it follows that, during the evidentiary hearing, the proportion of time liable to be devoted to cross-examination may be much higher in cases where the IBA Rules are applied.

To what extent, therefore, do the Rules seek to regulate cross-examination of witnesses generally, and experts in particular? The Rules deal with this question in some detail in Article 8, which focuses on the "evidentiary hearing".

Strictly speaking, however, many of the proposals they put forward are not "rules", but simply guidelines for the arbitrators to apply at their discretion. Thus, for example, *"The Arbitral tribunal may limit or exclude any question to, answer by or appearance of a witness... if it considers such question, answer or appearance to be irrelevant, immaterial, burdensome, duplicative..."* (Article 8.1).

However, even if the term "rules" is inappropriate, the content of Article 8.1 arguably goes as far as such a document can in seeking to help arbitrators settle the issue of which questions may be asked. And in fact, when it comes to deciding on the rules to apply to cross-examination, it should be noted that English civil procedure does not lay down a more rigid series of prescriptions to be followed!

The remaining provisions of Article 8 include guidelines as to how the questioning of witnesses is to be organised. It is noteworthy, however, that the IBA Rules nowhere seek to provide separate rules for oral evidence from experts as opposed to witnesses of fact.

Presumably no need was seen for any separate treatment, even for party experts/ expert witnesses who in some cases move from arbitration to arbitration, spending much more of their time advising in their expert-witness role than practising their profession, and no doubt able to offer training courses themselves on how to act as an expert and, in particular, deal with cross-examination!

CONCLUSION

Arbitration rules and practice generally recognise the common lawyers' concern to have an opportunity to interrogate party – or tribunal-appointed experts. However, party-appointed experts in particular are often well versed in the art of dealing with cross-examination, with the consequence that proper examination of such witnesses can be very time-consuming.

This in turn is incompatible with recent moves to speed up the arbitral process, and with limitations by arbitrators on the time available for the questioning of witnesses generally.

In fact, in practice, counsel will generally have to perform a balancing act – he or she will need to gauge the appropriate line of questioning to follow in view of the experience and expectation of the arbitrator, in other words according to the extent to which the arbitrator is likely to understand the cross-examination strategy being followed.

Would the situation be helped by more detailed rules? We would suggest that, on this specific issue as on many others, the solution lies instead with recourse to experienced arbitrators who are aware of the expectations of parties from different legal cultures, particularly when it comes to the question of how far counsel may go with his or her questions.

The oral evidence stage can only be enhanced by the use of arbitrators who are able to organize and control the hearing in a way that the parties are left with the feeling that principle of due process has been respected.

END NOTES

1 Peet v Mid-Kent Healthcare Trust [2002] 1 WLR 210.

2 See Section 34 of the Arbitration Act 1996.

3 See Article 1494 of the New Code of Civil Procedure.

4 See Article 20.4 of the ICC Rules.

5 See Article 20.3 of the ICC Rules.

6

Benefiting from oral testimony of expert witnesses:

Traditional and emerging techniques

By Richard H. Kreindler
Partner, Shearman & Sterling LLP, Germany
Council Member, ICC Institute of World Business Law

The subject of oral testimony by expert witnesses is one which is familiar to experienced disputes practitioners and laymen alike. Experienced arbitration counsel know well the potential importance of live testimony by an expert at a witness hearing, particularly in cases where the in-person response to questions is seized as an opportunity to simplify complex factual, technical and even legal matters in dispute. Non-lawyers and non-technical persons also have notional ideas of how crucial live testimony by experts can be, especially against the backdrop of the dramatization of the cross-examination of experts through the medium of Hollywood cinema. What these two differing, but overlapping perspectives clearly have in common is that the appearance of an expert in live proceedings can conceivably decide a dispute, and that the means of approaching such an encounter have continued to evolve over time.

The present brief *tour d'horizon* is couched in terms of "benefiting" from oral testimony of expert witnesses, and is divided into the following interrelated sections:

- General concepts applicable to expert oral testimony in international arbitration
- Orality of expert evidence and particular subject matter
- Selection of expert in arbitration for purposes of oral examination
- "Qualification" of the expert for purposes of oral examination

- Orality of expert testimony and the prior sequence of proceedings
- Possible options for oral examination of experts generally
- Goals of examination of expert witnesses from the perspective of the offering party
- Goals of examination of expert witnesses from the perspective of the opposing party
- Goals of examination of expert witnesses from the perspective of the arbitral tribunal
- Resulting means of benefiting from oral examination of expert witnesses

GENERAL CONCEPTS APPLICABLE TO EXPERT ORAL TESTIMONY IN INTERNATIONAL ARBITRATION

As a general conceptual overview, it is useful to divide the initial discussion of expert oral testimony in international arbitration into two broad categories: namely, (i) categories of experts per se and (ii) areas of oral (and written) testimony by experts.

This approach in the context of international arbitration could, substantially, also be applied to a discussion of use of experts in civil (and to a certain extent even criminal) litigation in the State courts. Indeed it is fair to say that many of the traditional, and especially emerging, approaches to the use of experts in international commercial and construction arbitration, especially in the common law jurisdictions, have their origins and inspiration in the ways in which experts are introduced into litigation proceedings. Similarly, in civil law jurisdictions, approaches to the use of experts in arbitration have, particularly in the past, likewise been influenced by the concept of experts in State court actions.

Three broad categories of expert might be identified. These are (i) the party-appointed expert, (ii) the tribunal-appointed expert designated with the consensus of parties, and (iii) the tribunal-appointed expert designated without the consensus of the parties.

In the case of party-appointed experts, modern-day, commonly used institutional and ad hoc arbitration regimes invariably provide for the introduction by one or more parties of expert evidence. In terms of the orality of such evidence, it is interesting to note certain commonly encountered differences in approach between common law- and civil law-inspired arbitration practitioners. For example, civil law-inspired statements of claim initiating an arbitration will often include "offers of evidence" with or without the name of a particular individual to serve as expert, whereas common law-inspired requests for arbitration more often stop short of making such offers on the theory that they are premature and that their absence should not be equated with an inability to substantiate the case.

In the former approach, where an expert or even a specific individual is introduced already in the first instance, presumably counsel will also have done the necessary due diligence before making the "offer" of the expert. With respect to the orality of the evidence, such inquiry should include (a) whether the expert evidence "lends itself" to oral examination and (b) whether the expert offered is suited to defend his expert opinion effectively under cross-examination.

Ultimately, the differences in approach with regard to the timing and specificity of offering expert evidence are increasingly becoming subject to convergence. Thus the stereotypical contrasts of earlier years are often breaking down. Alternatively, interestingly enough, common law practitioners may also partially adopt civil law approaches and civil law practitioners common law approaches, depending upon the needs of their particular case.

In the case of the tribunal-appointed expert designated with or without the consensus of the parties, the susceptibility of the taking of the expert evidence by oral means may be less of a concern, particularly where the tribunal selects the expert. In such cases, the tribunal would be well advised to preserve the ability to test the evidence of the expert by oral examination through the parties' counsel. At the same time, the tribunal may be less concerned with the expert's oral testimony than with his prior written report. In the case of a tribunal-appointed expert selected with the consensus and also the input or agreement of the parties, the concern may be greater.

Apart from the foregoing categories of experts per se, a general overview of oral expert evidence includes a sketch of possible areas of oral (and written) testimony by experts. It is fair to say that as time goes on and technology and commerce become more complex and interlinked, the areas of possible expert testimony likewise expand. Among the broad categories of possible expert testimony are construction, engineering, scientific, medical, intellectual property, econometric, accounting, environmental, psychological and legal. Such a list could be expanded at will, but in the context of oral expert testimony certain central points are worth making.

First, while some areas of expert testimony might appear to lend themselves more to oral examination than others, a competent expert (and competent counsel) can make even the most abstruse area of testimony come to life upon examination. By the same token, even the most straightforward area of expert testimony can become hopelessly tangled and unintelligible at the stage of oral testimony.

Second, inevitably, the nature of the contract is predetermined before the question arises of whether an expert is appropriate, and not the other way around. Thus the issue from counsel's and even the tribunal's point of view will normally be, does the particular dispute lend itself to examination at trial, or rather is it better dealt with, and even conclusively dealt with, on paper?

Third, in the case of an expert on issues of law, the problem of orality may be more complex even while the nature of the question would appear to be more accessible, especially to fellow lawyers. Particularly in the civil law tradition, the view is often expressed that an "expert" on law is either not required or a misnomer or both: the arbitral tribunal is deemed to be capable of ascertaining or taking notice of the law on its own. If the tribunal requires further assistance, it will resort to its own devices, but not be interested in an "expertise" on an issue under the applicable law.

In the common law tradition, on the other hand, there is nothing per se untoward about offering a professor or practitioner as an expert of law, and such testimony can be considered as testimony of fact to be assessed by the tribunal along with any and all other evidence on facts. In this context, it may not be surprising that many common law-inspired tribunals have a greater openness to oral examination of experts of law than do civil law-motivated tribunals.

ORALITY OF EXPERT EVIDENCE AND PARTICULAR SUBJECT MATTER

A further refinement might be made by approaching oral testimony of experts not solely by category of subject matter, but by (i) susceptibility to oral examination and explanation and (ii) dependence of the expert testimony on written documentation and data.

In the case of the first perspective, susceptibility to oral examination and explanation, one might posit four broad categories of experts who would be subject to oral examination: (a) experts who calculate, (b) experts who test, measure or reconstruct, (c) experts who challenge how someone else did something, and (d) experts who opine on the state of the law. At first glance, it might be supposed that experts who challenge how someone else did something would be most usefully subject to oral examination, but of course this depends on the nature and category of activity of the person whom the expert is second-guessing (or confirming).

In the case of experts who calculate, the calculations on their own may not benefit greatly from oral examination, but of course the overall demeanour and credibility of the expert confirming or denying the calculations may be better scrutinized if subject to live testimony.

The same observation would surely apply to any other category of expert examination, including opinions of law. There, the benefit of the oral examination might be seen less in the added value of demonstrating the way the opinion was reached than in the opportunity to size up the witness' overall likelihood to be telling the truth and expressing a true expert view.

In the case of the second perspective, the dependence of expert testimony on written documentation and data, a high dependence on the written word as the basis for the expert conclusions need not necessarily mean that oral examination on those same conclusions would be useless, impracticable or both.

Again, in most cases other than eyewitness disputes revolving around events (such as accidents) or representations (such as promises), the dispute will depend upon certain writings, and perhaps on only a very few. In those disputes, such as many construction matters, the voluminous drawings, change orders, variations, schedule diagrams and the like cannot be reduced to less than several hundred despite best efforts. There, it may be precisely the oral synthesis of the expert which assists the tribunal to make sense of the written collage.

Various kinds of written documentation or data may impact on the later use of oral expert testimony.

First, correspondence and contemporaneous records will exist in most cases, especially those involving disputes between sophisticated parties and particularly in the construction and accounting fields.

Second, also in the construction field, site visits or other physical inspection may be called for, and may result in a kind of oral examination of experts which is significantly influenced by the presence of demonstrable evidence not in the hearing room, but on site for all to see. Such site visits can conceivably take place with or without the participation of the parties, or even with or without the participation of the tribunal. However, in the case of a lack of participation, normally no real oral examination can take place while preserving the requirements of due process.

Third, written documentation might also consist of photos, videos and other visual inspection, which will call for or lend itself to oral examination of expert witnesses.

Fourth, such documentation might take the form of empirical studies, analyses and calculations or of maps, diagrams and drawings, as to which an expert opinion may be best expressed by means of oral testimony.

Fifth, in many cases, expert testimony is sought to be supported by machine-made or hand-made representations, on which the expert, particularly under direct examination, bases his oral evidence. Depending upon the subject matter and the backgrounds of the members of the arbitral tribunal, such reliance on "demonstrable evidence" may be considered a true benefit, or may be perceived as an unnecessary and exaggerated dramatization of the issues.

SELECTION OF EXPERT IN ARBITRATION FOR PURPOSES OF ORAL EXAMINATION

Generally, the question of whether to select an expert and whom to select for purposes of oral examination might be seen in two broad senses.

In those cases where the expert's oral testimony is to be preceded by the expert's written expert report or affidavit, the expert will normally set out the justification for holding himself out as such in writing. Any scrutiny of whether such person truly is an expert, and an expert in a relevant field, will normally best take place in subsequent oral examination, if any.

If it is unclear or unlikely that such oral examination will in fact take place, then the expert and the party putting him forward must use the written expert report as the one and possibly only opportunity to justify his standing as expert. In this regard, the cultural, legal and other background of the party and of the would-be expert may influence how such opportunity is used.

Among the many differences which may arise here, a classical one is the so-called "hired gun," that is, the expert who may be perceived as being prepared to advocate an opinion dictated to him as long as he is remunerated adequately for such exercise.

In reality, the alacrity with which many civil law observers criticize Anglo-American use of experts as indulging in battles of hired guns is often misplaced and unjustified. A well-prepared expert in the one culture is not necessarily any less independent than in the other culture. Both are remunerated for their services. Both have reputations to protect. Both must be prepared to withstand cross-examination. The institutionalization of expert testimony in the common law systems results in a higher frequency of abuse of the system as a result of the higher number of would-be experts generally. At the same time, it also results in a higher degree of professionalism in certain respects than is encountered with certain experts in the civil law realm.

Second, the question of whether to select an expert and whom to select for purposes of oral examination might be seen as a function of the particular arbitration. In this regard, the degree of orality of the arbitration is of course central.

Some arbitrations, particularly in the domestic English realm, are "documents-only" proceedings with essentially no oral testimony and even little or no oral advocacy by counsel. The case can be made that many arbitrations could just as well be conducted with a just result on the basis of documents, and with far less cost and time. At the same time, the parties will often disagree as to whether the arbitration can be conducted in this manner, based in part on differing views of the benefits of oral testimony to their respective case. Also, such views may not always be formed at an early stage.

Apart from the somewhat extreme example of documents-only arbitrations, which are in principle rare in large commercial disputes, the orality of expert testimony must also be seen in the context of the qualifications and knowledge of the tribunal members. Depending upon their respective technical and/or legal knowledge and what knowledge is called for to decide the dispute, a party may favour or disfavour oral examination of his experts or opposing experts.

A well-organized party who already has his experts in place at an early stage of the arbitration may in fact allow his selection of a party-designated arbitrator and of the chairman be influenced by the selection he has already made of an expert. If he has determined that an expert is crucial and that the person chosen would best be given a stage for extensive questioning by the tribunal, he may also wish to ensure that the members of the tribunal are persons who would be most suited to conducting such questioning.

In reverse order, if the tribunal has already been selected and only later is a determination made that oral expert testimony would advance the cause, the selection of a particular individual as expert may be guided by the degree of sophistication, or lack thereof, of the tribunal members already in office as to the issue about which the expert would opine.

Yet a further variation on the foregoing which may also influence the selection of the expert-witness is the extent to which an advance definition of the expert issues has been achieved, either by contractually stipulated mechanism or by agreement among the parties after commencement of the arbitration or by dictate of the tribunal.

In the presence of such a list, the parties may be able to make a more focused decision as to which person is appropriate as expert, and whether his oral testimony would be productive in adjudicating specific issues. In the absence of such a list, the parties may be less able to make a focused decision, may feel obliged to have a more widely ranging expert opinion, and may be less comfortable determining whether that opinion would be aided or undermined by scrutiny in the form of oral examination.

"QUALIFICATION" OF EXPERT FOR PURPOSES OF ORAL EXAMINATION

The use of oral expert testimony in international arbitration is partly a function of whether the person put forward as an expert actually "qualifies" as one. Four observations may be made in this regard.

First, the qualification of the would-be expert as an "expert" may normally be based on one or more of (i) knowledge, (ii) skill, (iii) experience, and (iv) training and education.

Normally, the ability of the expert and of the party putting him forward to ensure a successful qualification as expert in the estimation of the tribunal should not depend critically on whether the person is subject to oral examination. On the other hand, as stated above, depending upon the circumstances the opportunity of oral examination and inquiry may be conducive to solidifying the conclusion that the expert is qualified based on one or more of the foregoing bases.

The determination of whether oral testimony would have added value in this regard may also be a function of which person has been put forward by the opposing party as a counterpoised expert, and whether oral examination would be likely to place that counterpoised expert in a more or a less favourable light.

Second, the knowledge or skill being relied upon to qualify as expert need not be formal or academic. This recognition by itself may also influence whether oral examination is perceived to be critical to the qualification as an expert.

At least two corollaries follow from this observation. On the one hand, the absence of experience need not be disqualifying and on the other hand, stellar qualifications must still match the subject matter of the expert testimony.

Third, the "qualification" as an expert is ultimately within the discretion of the arbitral tribunal. The exercise of that discretion is linked to the overall discretion of the tribunal to weigh and assess the evidence. In some cases, the exercise of that discretion may be reviewable on one or more of the grounds available for seeking annulment of the award at the seat of arbitration, but bearing in mind how stringent the standards applied to such petitions normally are.

Fourth, when considering the desirability of oral testimony by the expert as a part of the decision of whom to select as expert, it should be borne in mind that the ultimate contribution of the expert may be more one of "synthesis" and "assimilation" than of providing a reliable opinion.

While the true role of the expert is to provide an expert opinion, it may not be until late in the arbitration that it becomes apparent that the greatest service rendered by the expert has been one of organizing, digesting and depicting the main issues in order to render his opinion, while his opinion per se is less useful. This synthesis and assimilation function will most likely have taken place through submission of the written expert report. However, as mentioned above it is entirely possible that oral testimony can also play such a role, even in the case of a voluminous prior documentary record.

ORALITY OF EXPERT TESTIMONY AND THE PRIOR SEQUENCE OF PROCEEDINGS

The extent to which oral expert testimony may be useful or desirable in the arbitration proceedings may also depend on what has already transpired in the arbitration, before the decision has been made.

In the context of US-style and US-venued arbitration, depositions may be foreseen or may already have taken place as part of the taking of evidence. Depending upon the procedure agreed or otherwise dictated, such depositions would normally occur before the submission of witness statements, including expert reports.

In such a case, the depositions may play a critical role in determining the extent of later oral examination of an expert who was subject to deposition. As a function of how well the expert acquitted himself under deposition, he may or may not be asked to put forward a written expert report. Also as a function of the deposition, the scope of any such report may be circumscribed or otherwise altered, and thus the scope of his later oral examination may be affected.

Such decisions would not be able to be made without the benefit of the depositions, and in this respect this oft-maligned evidentiary vehicle often actually plays a useful role in focusing and tailoring the later proceedings relating to experts.

Furthermore, written expert reports may be exchanged simultaneously or consecutively, in one round or two. This framework may likewise influence the content and scope of the written report, and thereby of any later oral examination.

Whether or not expert reports are simultaneous or consecutive, their scope may also be defined, as mentioned above, by party agreement, terms of reference or a procedural order, thereby impacting on the usefulness and scope of any subsequent oral examination.

In some cases, the parties agree or the tribunal determines that the experts shall answer a questionnaire of remaining issues in advance of an oral hearing. In other cases, a list of "undisputed issues" and a list of "disputed issues" may be generated on the basis of the competing expert reports, thereby clarifying what the remaining points for discussion must be under oral examination from the tribunal's point of view.

Finally, an increasingly relevant aspect of determining whether and how to have expert testimony under oral examination is the existence of a prior or parallel expert determination on accounting, tax or price adjustment issues. In some cases, an expert determination will already have taken place and form a final and binding part of the scope of the expert's report in the arbitration. In other cases, the expert determination will not have taken place due to competing claims of competence of the expert determination and the expert in the arbitration.

In either such case, it may make sense for the expert in the arbitration to have a full opportunity to set forth his views before the tribunal, if also so as to enable it to determine whether it has jurisdiction over the matter at hand.

POSSIBLE OPTIONS FOR ORAL EXAMINATION OF EXPERTS GENERALLY

Having made a determination that oral examination of an expert is in principle desirable or tolerable, the examination itself may take one or more various forms.

First, as mentioned, often in arbitrations at least in the United States, there may be deposition of experts in advance of the hearing before the tribunal. In such a case, one issue at trial upon examination of the expert will be that of the consistency between the expert's written report, his deposition testimony and his testimony before the tribunal.

Second, the question of "direct examination" and "cross-examination" by counsel may arise. Even if the procedural directions in the arbitration indicate that the prior written expert report is in lieu of direct examination, there may be substantial "redirect" examination, and the expert may seek to make extensive statements even in response to the cross-examination by opposing counsel.

Third, there may be more or less inquisitorial examination of the expert-witness by the arbitral tribunal. There may be a mixture of examination by counsel and the tribunal. There may also be "witness conferencing" of experts simultaneously present in the hearing room and conducting effectively a dialogue on specific issues and questions in front of the parties and tribunal. Further possibilities include questioning of party-appointed experts by each other or by a tribunal-appointed expert.

In any and all such cases, the parties and their experts should enjoy as much clarity as possible before the hearing as to the expectations and possibilities for oral testimony from the standpoint of the tribunal. If such clarity is not achieved, even the most reputable and coherent expert-witness may become unhinged. Alternatively, his voice may otherwise go under, in the procedural chaos which may emerge when the parties do not agree on the format and ground rules for the witness examination.

GOALS OF ORAL EXAMINATION OF EXPERT-WITNESS FROM THE PERSPECTIVE OF THE OFFERING PARTY

Among the objectives of the party offering the expert for examination, at least three principal areas come to mind.

First, the offering party has the desire, and the need, to qualify the expert-witness as an expert – most particularly in the eyes of the arbitral tribunal, but perhaps no less in the eyes of the opposing party and also the counterpoised expert, if any, of the opposing party.

Such qualification can be achieved in a number of different ways, and in some situations is brief, uncomplicated and perhaps all but unnecessary. In other cases, qualification is less clear or in any event requires a series of steps to be achieved before the witness is at least nominally considered to be an expert.

Of course, in contradistinction to the somewhat formalistic approach of "qualifying" an expert in civil litigation in the United States under the Federal Rules of Evidence, the qualification process in an international arbitration can be much more free-flowing and fluid, or indeed not take place at all. Alternatively, the effort to establish the witness as an "expert" may parallel some of the same steps in the rituals of the Federal Rules of Evidence, but the arbitral tribunal will see no need to formally acknowledge that the qualification has succeeded before proceeding with the examination of that witness.

Whatever method is employed, the "qualification" as expert will obviously rely in the first instance on one or more of the witness' training, experience, prior research or observations, etc.

Second, qualification of the person as an expert need not guarantee that such person is "the right person" to provide an expert opinion on the issue or issues which the offering party claims would benefit from, or depend on, an opinion from an expert.

In other words, even if that person is shown to have a particular expertise, the offering party would do well to make use of the oral examination of the witness to demonstrate that the subject of his or her testimony is directly linked to his expert experience or knowledge, and that such testimony is relevant and material to the issue in dispute. In those oral examinations where, increasingly, the prior written witness statement is deemed to be in lieu of direct examination, this goal will necessarily need to be achieved in the course of cross-examination, interrogation by the tribunal, re-direct examination and, if any, witness conferencing with the opposing expert.

Third, a witness who appears to be an expert and whose testimony appears to be material and relevant to an issue in dispute must still normally establish a sound and prevailing basis for the forming of such opinion.

Even the most esteemed expert whose expertise would appear to fall squarely into the area of dispute may come across as unhelpful to the task of the arbitral tribunal if, on oral examination, he is not able to demonstrate an appropriate basis for having reached his particular opinion. In this respect, depending upon the case and the nature of the expertise, there may be one or more tenable bases for the opinion, including, e.g., (i) facts or data personally perceived by the expert, (ii) hearsay which the tribunal decides nonetheless to admit, (iii) facts or data not personally perceived but reasonably relied upon, and (iv) facts or data communicated to the expert only at the hearing.

In the context of the goals of oral examination from the standpoint of the party offering the expert, there are a host of other issues which are relevant to the direct examination. These may include the acceptable and effective use of demonstrative aids or evidence as part of the qualification process, the characterization of the expert as an expert of law or rather as an expert of fact, and the issue of whether the expert may attend some or all of the witness hearing and oral argument not strictly related to his own testimony, and in particular before he has been examined. Depending upon the circumstances and the proclivities of the parties and the tribunal, these issues may be decided in quite different ways.

GOALS OF ORAL EXAMINATION OF EXPERT-WITNESS FROM THE PERSPECTIVE OF THE OPPOSING PARTY

Among the objectives of the party opposing the expert for examination, the considerations are to a large extent the mirror-image of the three principal areas just mentioned.

Thus, **first**, the opposing party may seek to disqualify the witness *ab initio* as an expert. Such consideration may depend on whether the effort to do so is credible and achievable, and whether such person's testimony even if accepted as being expert is, in the view of the opposing party, germane to the case.

Not every attempt to disqualify an expert is worth undertaking, or even dispositive of the dispute. When such attempt to "disqualify," if made, should take place will depend upon the particular procedural modalities agreed upon or dictated by the tribunal. Where the expert has submitted a prior written report, it is possible that the opposing party will have submitted a competing expert report at the same time or subsequently which may set out to undermine the qualifications of the other expert. In international arbitration, this would appear to be infrequent, however, and in most situations the effort to disqualify is left to counsel and not made part of the task of the counter-poised expert. Thus the effort to disqualify, if undertaken, will instead be made by counsel upon cross-examination at the hearing.

Second, counsel for the opposing party may see fit to discredit the link between the subject of the testimony and the specific expertise. In such case, again usually on cross-examination, a good-faith effort might be made to establish to the arbitral tribunal that while the expert is technically qualified, his qualification has little or nothing to do with the opinion which he seeks to give and seeks to characterize as being expert.

Third, the opposing party will frequently seek not so much to disqualify the expert or to challenge the link between his knowledge and his testimony, but rather to discredit the "basis" for the opinion which he offers.

The same general categories of possible basis for an expert opinion may be relevant here. Thus on cross-examination counsel may seek to establish that the facts or data on which the expert relied to form his opinion were actually not personally perceived by the expert, or that he relied on hearsay or other evidence which should not be admitted. Other possible means of discrediting on cross-examination may include that the facts and data were not only not personally perceived, but also not reasonably relied on because they were statistically nonrepresentative, etc. In the case of facts or data communicated to the expert only at the hearing, the expert may be particularly susceptible to discrediting if he is unable to present a reasonable basis for assimilating such facts or data. On the other hand, the very fact that the basis was provided only at the hearing will often be factored in by the arbitral tribunal in assessing and weighing the testimony.

Other issues are relevant to the cross-examination of the expert or would-be expert. These include objectionable use of demonstrative aids and motions to exclude the presence of the expert before and/or after his specific witness testimony.

Also, particularly in arbitrations involving US counsel and/or US experts, there may be disputes as to whether the expert is impermissibly declining to answer a question or reveal the factual or documentary basis for forming his opinion on the grounds of attorney-client or attorney-work product privileges, or even somewhat analogous protections available in other legal systems.

Finally, particularly in the case of an expert opinion of law, cross-examination may revolve on the objection that the testimony is of little or no use in any event, since under the principle of *jura novit curia* the arbitral tribunal is deemed to know, and have its own means of verifying, the applicable law without extrinsic testimony.

GOALS OF EXAMINATION OF THE EXPERT-WITNESS FROM THE PERSPECTIVE OF THE ARBITRAL TRIBUNAL

Ultimately, neither the expert-witness himself nor the party or counsel offering or opposing him can afford to lose sight of what the arbitral tribunal hopes to benefit from his oral examination.

This holds true irrespective of whether the tribunal takes a more inquisitorial and dirigistic approach, conducting the examination substantially on its own, or instead leaves the examination largely or wholly to the parties' counsel and passively follows the questioning. Particularly in the latter case, counsel and the expert must be all the more attentive to what the arbitral tribunal is likely to need and to want to know as a result of the expert testimony. This is especially the case if the arbitral tribunal offers few overt "cues" as to what parts of the competing expert testimonies most concern it. In this regard, a number of possible goals on the part of the arbitral tribunal may be identified.

First, as a matter of efficiency and evidentiary weighting, the arbitral tribunal will normally indeed wish to make conclusions as to whether the witness offered can be qualified as an expert.

Second, cross-examination and questioning by the arbitral tribunal itself can and should serve the goal of determining which questions really depend upon expert input and cannot be responsibly answered without it – as opposed to simply being "embellished" by the testimony of an expert as "icing on the cake."

Third, what is the relevant training and experience for a probative expert input on the subject in dispute? Questioning by the tribunal in this regard, including querying counsel on why they have put forward a particular expert, may serve to answer such a question.

Fourth, the arbitral tribunal may question whether the expert opinion being proffered actually needs to be communicated orally, or whether it is even susceptible of being communicated orally. Depending upon the complexity and nature of the underlying subject matter and the explication of the expert opinion, it could be that the prior written expert report is deemed to be sufficient, and even superior to any attempts to elaborate upon its content orally.

Fifth, the basis for the expert opinion reached should typically be a concern for the arbitral tribunal in the course of the oral examination. Does the witness possess the relevant expertise, does he possess the relevant and correct facts and data, and does he appear to have relied upon the same to reach his expert conclusion?

Sixth, in this regard oral examination may also be conducive to establishing whether any disagreement between competing experts is based on the same objective features and data, or rather on two different universes of information. If such differences are shown or assumed to exist and are critical to the case, witness conferencing in which both experts are questioned about the underlying facts and data at the same time may assist in narrowing the differences of opinion.

Seventh, where two experts appear to have been working from substantially the same baseline and the disagreement between them persists into and during the oral examination, the questioning in person may serve to explore whether such disagreement is actually relevant to the adjudication of the dispute. Some disagreements may not bear upon the central issue. Others do, and the oral questioning may help to determine whether in fact the disagreement can be reconciled by the tribunal based on other considerations, including common sense, without having to "choose between" the two opinions.

Eighth, particularly in complex construction and infrastructure disputes, elaborate demonstrative aids (charts, timelines, photographs, plotplans, blue-prints, etc.) may be relied upon in the course of the oral examination of an expert-witness. The expert and counsel must at all times ask themselves whether such aids are truly helpful, or instead are even harmful and counter-productive to the cause of communicating a particular opinion to the arbitral tribunal. This inquiry will largely be a function of the nature of the opinion together with the backgrounds of the members of the tribunal.

Finally, the issue of privilege may surface. Attorney-client, attorney work-product and other privileges or legal impediments to participation in the taking of evidence may be of just as great importance to the tribunal as to the counsel invoking them – or they may be considered to be more in the nature of a side-show. Clearly, the tribunal has an obligation to consider the legitimacy of the invocation of a privilege as part of its mandate to observe due process and equal treatment. In the context of oral examination of expert witnesses, the arbitral tribunal may have to decide, even spontaneously, whether to accept or to ignore the invocation of a privilege in midstream during oral examination. Counsel would be well advised to ensure that the tribunal has the complete factual and legal basis for understanding the arguments made about privilege, so that they can be properly assessed during and after the oral examination of the expert-witness.

RESULTING MEANS OF BENEFITING FROM ORAL EXAMINATION OF EXPERT WITNESSES

In view of the foregoing, it is apparent that the contours and usefulness of an oral examination of expert witnesses in international arbitration will depend upon a number of factors. These will of course include the parties, counsel, arbitrators and experts involved. They will also include any applicable or perceived procedural and other confines relevant to the way in which the oral examination is conducted.

Since certain imponderables will always apply to an oral examination, it is all the more important to attempt to attach as much transparency as possible to the process, and at the earliest sensible stage. Initial procedural orders may seek to regulate the use of expert witnesses at trial in detail from the outset of the arbitration. Still, it is entirely possible that such regulations will need to be revisited as the character of the arbitration becomes clearer and more tangible in the succeeding weeks and months.

Whatever the timing, it is critical that well before going into the examination of the expert witnesses, all participants concerned have a concrete understanding of what the ground rules are, what the expectations on all sides should be, and what flexibility may still obtain and be taken advantage of in the oral examination. While this would speak in favour of addressing such issues at an early stage, it is also likely that any rules agreed upon at the beginning of the arbitration may need to be revisited or confirmed later on, as the witness hearing approaches.

If such due diligence and good housekeeping, so to speak, are observed on all sides and most particularly by a vigilant arbitral tribunal, it is likely that the oral examination of the expert witnesses may be useful, probative and instrumental to the assessing of the one or other critical point leading to either settlement or adjudication by award. It is also likely that differences in approach to the oral examination of expert witnesses – based in part on cultural, educational and philosophical divides – can be bridged to at least some extent to accommodate the competing needs of the participants in an international arbitration.

7

Counsel-witness relations and professional misconduct in civil law systems

(Published in 2003 by Arbitration International Vol. 19, 457 and re-published here by kind permission)

*By Hans van Houtte**

In order to understand the counsel-witness relations in civil law arbitrations one first needs to understand how civil law courts handle witnesses whereby the parties' counsel is in a supporting role. Indeed, the arbitration statutes in civil law countries envisage that arbitrators will deal with witnesses in the same way as judges do, with counsel as mere "walk-ons". However, in practice – and under Anglo-American influence – counsel in civil law arbitrations play an active role in the presentation of witness evidence – an approach that stands at right angles to the civil law legal tradition. As this phenomenon is rather new, the civil lawyer's code of ethics does not yet fully address misconduct in counsel-witness relations in the margin of arbitration proceedings. However, a few basic rules are surely relevant.

THE CIVIL LAW TRADITION

1. State courts

It is an essential feature of civil law proceedings that the courts assume the obligation to investigate the case themselves and to find the "truth".

In the past, civil law courts investigated a case without any contribution of counsel; not only in criminal matters, but also in civil and commercial matters.

---

* FCI Arb., Institute for International Trade Law, Louvain University, Belgium, hans.vanhoutte@law.kuleuven.ac.be

A 19th century French avocat was for instance not allowed to interfere with the court's "*instruction de l'affaire*" in a commercial dispute. When the court heard a witness, the avocat could thus not attend the hearing. A fortiori should he not visit prospective witnesses to learn what they had to say and – surely not – influence their statement[1]. The rules, undoubtedly, have become less strict. Nevertheless, some of the underlying philosophy has somehow survived. Indeed, nowadays, civil law courts still see it as their task to lead the investigation of the case.

However in most continental European countries (e.g. Austria[2], Germany[3], the Netherlands[4] , Sweden[5]) counsel may approach and meet a prospective witness. In Belgium, France, Italy[6] and Switzerland[7], on the other hand, the Rules of Conduct of the Bar still forbid counsel to interview prospective witnesses[8].

In fact, however, in civil and commercial court proceedings, witnesses are not much used. They are of secondary importance. For civil matters, the Code Napoleon Article 1341, for instance, has significantly curbed the possibility to use witness testimony to contradict written documents. Although the same strict rule does not exist for commercial matters, where witness evidence is more generally admitted[9], in commercial matters also witness testimony is rarely submitted. For instance, in thirty years of commercial litigation, I have had only two instances where a Belgian court had heard witnesses.

Moreover, if a witness nonetheless has to be heard, in most civil law countries the courts have kept a preponderant – if not exclusive – role: it is the judge who examins the witness. Generally, neither the parties nor their counsel have the opportunity to question the witness directly. A party usually forwards its questions to the judge, who then has full discretion in deciding to put the question to the witness. In many jurisdictions, the parties and their counsel cannot even interrupt a witness[10].

2. Arbitration

Traditionally witnesses had a similar minor role in civil law arbitration. Arbitrators restricted witness evidence in the same way as courts did. A Belgian arbitration treatise thus admonished arbitrators to admit witness evidence in civil and commercial matters only when the law allowed for such evidence[11]. In fact, witnesses were only used in arbitration when there was no written evidence available[12]. It is for instance also quite striking that a leading French treaty on arbitration, Jean Robert's *L'arbitrage*, in its 1983 edition, did not discuss witness evidence at all.

Whenever arbitrators hear witnesses, they follow as much as possible the same modalities as a court would do. Depending on the applicable arbitration law, they administer an oath[13]; they exclude as witness persons with too close a link to the parties; they and not the parties question the witness and draft minutes of the hearing[14]. Arbitrators – or even only one of them – sometimes examine the witnesses in the absence of the parties and their counsel. (In that event, the arbitrators will submit a *"procès-verbal"* of the examination to the parties so that they are aware of its outcome)[15]. Whenever a witness would refuse to appear before the arbitrators, depending on the applicable law, the State court either can order the witness to appear before the arbitral tribunal, or can question the witness itself[16].

PRESENT ARBITRATION PRACTICE

In their sociological exploration of the arbitration world, Dezelay and Garth described how Anglo-American lawyers, who play a preponderant role in present-day-arbitration, have modelled their international arbitration proceedings on their US court practice and have turned transnational arbitration into some offshore US-style litigation[17]. The intensive reliance on witnesses and their cross-examination by counsel is part of this change. At first some European arbitrators considered cross-examination of witnesses "barbaric" and "primitive". Others, however, soon "began to realize that parties seemed to like this cross-examination" and were open to this new approach[18].

Consequently, in Europe also witnesses are now becoming a substantial element in arbitration proceedings; not only for transatlantic or cross-channel cases, but also for Continental European disputes and even for purely domestic disputes. Occasionally, a Continental European arbitrator may still insist that it will be him – and not counsel – who will put the questions to the witness; that implies that counsel does not question the witness in direct and cross-examination but can only prompt the Chairman of the Tribunal with the questions the latter will put to the witness – a rather boring, denigrating and time-consuming exercise. After a few questions, however, reasonableness generally prevails over formality and counsel addresses the witness directly.

For modern Continental European arbitrators, witness evidence, production of witness lists, submission of witness statements, examination in chief, cross-examination, re-examination and re-cross have become an inherent part of the arbitration proceedings. The IBA Rules on Evidence in International Commercial Arbitration, meant in the first instance to bridge procedural gaps between civil and common law i.e. on the presentation of evidence, are often also used for intra-continental European disputes – and even in purely domestic arbitrations.

In brief, Continental European arbitrators, rooted in the inquisitorial tradition, have discovered the benefits of adversarial questioning. That allows many of them to combine the best of the Continental European tradition with Anglo-American approaches. In a first stage they often will thus allow counsel to address the witnesses; at the end they may themselves question the witness directly. Some European arbitrators, not preconditioned by preconceived axioms, also embark on efficient "witness conferencing", where witnesses, counsel and parties are collectively confronted with the relevant issues[19].

COUNSEL-WITNESS RELATIONSHIP IN TRANSNATIONAL ARBITRATION

Party-witnesses are a relatively recent phenomenon in Continental European arbitration. There is not yet an extensive Code of Ethics on the relationship between counsel and witness. Nevertheless a few salient issues have to be addressed.

- **Is it permissible for European counsel to interview prospective witnesses?**

The IBA Rules of Evidence, that aim to introduce worldwide arbitration standards, are not of much help. They do not forbid preliminary contacts when European counsel is involved in an international arbitration. However, neither do they endorse the practice. They merely state that "*It shall not be improper for a Party, its officers, employees, legal advisors and other representatives to interview its witnesses or potential witnesses*". These IBA Rules that set procedural rules, in fact are less relevant to determine standards for professional conduct. They have no bearing on the Code of Ethics to which counsel in their respective countries are subjected. More relevant therefore is what the local bar rules and standards of professional ethics allow for.

Even in countries (e.g. in Belgium, France[20], Italy[21] and Switzerland[22]) where counsel is not permitted to contact prospective witnesses in court litigation, he may contact witnesses for a transnational arbitration. For instance, the Deontologicial Code of the Brussels Bar provides that counsel should avoid all contact with witnesses. However, it explicitly provides that these rules do not apply to foreign or transnational arbitration whenever such contacts are permitted under the rules governing that arbitration[23].

■ May a Continental European counsel also "coach" his witnesses?

Such practice seems to be accepted in some countries (e.g. the Netherlands), but not in others (e.g. Belgium). Nevertheless, many European arbitrators are reluctant and discourage such coaching. An experienced arbitrator like Piet Sanders for instance is very clear on this issue:

> "Drawn up with the party or its legal advisors the witness may be influenced in formulating his or her Statement which has to be signed and affirmed by him or her as being the truth. In my opinion these Witness Statements, preceding the hearings of the witnesses in person, are not in accordance with the expectations of many parties in an international arbitration"[24].

However in all events equality between the parties requires that all the parties and their counsel apply the same standards. To that end arbitrators should for instance make clear in the Terms of Reference or in the pre-hearing conference whether counsel are allowed to contact – and even coach – the witnesses.

■ May counsel contact the other party's witness?

In the Continental Europe legal tradition it is already a daring step for counsel in arbitration to contact (and prepare) his own witnesses. The possibility that he could also contact the other party's witness probably goes beyond counsel's imagination. Therefore, not many Codes of Ethics address such flagrant misbehaviour. As far as I know only the Dutch Code of Ethics explicitly forbids counsel prior to the hearing to contact witnesses from the other side.

In fact, the same prohibition can be deducted from the so called "CCBE Code of Conduct", established by the Bars from the European Union[25] where it says:

> "A lawyer shall not communicate about a particular case or matter directly with any person whom he knows to be represented or advised in the case or matter by another lawyer, without the consent of that other lawyer (and shall keep the other lawyer informed of any such communication)" (Art. 5.5).

If a counsel cannot communicate with the adverse party behind its counsel's back, he by analogy is not entitled to do so with the witness put forward by that counsel.

Similarly, a prohibition to contact the other party's witness follows from Art. 4.3 of the IBA Rules of Evidence: "*It shall not be improper ... to interview its witnesses or potential witnesses*". If the interview of one's own witnesses has to allowed expressly, communications with the other party's witnesses seem to be forbidden *a contrario*.

■ What are the sanctions for attempting to influence witnesses?

Of course, arbitrators who are aware that a witness has been influenced, will attach less or no weight to his testimony. As the IBA Rules of Evidence (Article 9.1) confirm: "*The arbitral tribunal shall determine the ... weight of the evidence*".

Moreover, counsel who has tried to influence a witness may be subject to the disciplinary sanction of his own Bar Authorities[26]. Furthermore, he may be subject to criminal prosecution because of fraud[27] or obstruction of justice[28]. The award may be set aside because of a breach of public policy[29]. Enforcement of the award may be refused for the same reason.

In transnational arbitrations counsel often come from different jurisdictions. Is each of them bound by his own rules so that their respective professional standards may be different? It is hereby suggested that, in transnational arbitration, counsel's professional conduct has to conform to a double standard.

In all events, it has to comply with the standards of the country where the seat of the arbitration is located. Indeed, within the European Union, the professional standards of the place where proceedings are held apply also to attorneys coming from a different jurisdiction. The CCBE Code of Conduct (Art. 4.1) states this explicitly for court proceedings: "*A lawyer who appears or takes part in a case before a court or tribunal in a Member State must comply with the rules of conduct applied before that court or tribunal*". The same applies to arbitration proceedings: "*The rules governing a lawyer's relationship with the courts apply also to his relations with arbitrators ...*" *(Art. 5.4)*.

Consequently, whenever the seat of the arbitration is within the European Union, the standards of the seat of arbitration apply[30]. Although the CCBE claims no authority to regulate counsel's behaviour outside the European Union, one should assume that the principle it endorsed also applies whenever the seat of arbitration is outside the E.U.

In addition, a counsel cannot be exempted from his own professional standards. If those standards are different, they have to be attuned to come to a workable compromise. Arbitrators should be aware of the possible discrepancy between counsels' professional standards and address this matter in a pre-hearing conference or in possible Terms of Reference.

END NOTES

1 M. Cresson, Usages et Règles de la Profession d'Avocat, Vol. 2, Paris, 1888, 20.

2 See C. Liebscher and A. Schmid, "Austria" in F.B. Weigand, ed., Practitioner's Handbook on International Arbitration, Beck München, 2002, 563.

3 See G. Wagner, "Germany", in F.B. Weigand, ed., *o.c.*, 756.

4 See V. Lazic and G. Meijer, "Netherlands" in F.B. Weigand, ed., *o.c,* 921.

5 See K. Hober and H. Strempel, "Sweden" in F.B. Weigand, ed., *o.c,*1027.

6 See M. Rubino-Sammartano, "Italy" in F.B. Weigand, ed., o.c, 857.

7 See P. Karrer and P. Straub, "Switzerland" in F.B. Weigand, ed., o.c, 1063.

8 See the country reports in J.P. Lachmann, Handbüch für Schiedsgerichtspraxis, Cologne 1998.

9 See, e.g., Belgian Cass. May 7, 1908; "Except when excluded by statutes in commercial matters witness evidence can go against or beyond the content of documents".

10 See, e.g., Belgian Code Judiciaire, Articles 936-938.

11 A. Bernard, L'arbitrage volontaire en droit privé, Brussels, 1937, No. 414.

12 See R. Perrot, L'administration de la preuve en matière d'arbitrage, Rev. Arb., 1974, 159, 165.

13 Not in France, CCP Art. 1441.

14 A. Bernard, o.c., nr. 414; Garsonnet et Cézar-Bru, Traité theorique et pratique de procédure civile et commerciale, 3d ed., Paris 1923., Vol. VIII, No. 280.

15 See, e.g., French CCP Art. 263; M. De Boisséson, Le droit français de l'arbitrage, Paris, 1983, 253.

16 See, e.g., the Netherlands, CCP Art. 1041 (2); Belgium: CCP Art. 1696 (2). In Denmark and Germany (ZPO § 1050) the arbitrators may participate in the court hearing and ask questions.

17 Y. Dezalay and G. Garth, Dealing in Virtue, Chicago, 1996, 53.

18 Dezalay and Garth, o.c., 53.

19 See, e.g., W. Peter, "Witness Conferencing" Arb. Int., 2002, 47.

20 "France" in F.B. Weigand, ed., o.c, 663.

21 See M. Rubino Sammartano, "Italy" in F.B. Weigand, ed., o.c, 857.

22 See P. Karrer and P. Straub, "Switzerland" in F.B. Weigand, ed., o.c, 1063.

23 See Articles 5 and 16.8.

24 Sanders, Quo Vadis Arbitration? Sixty Years of Arbitration Practice, Kluwer, 1999, 262.

25 CCBE stands for Comité Consultatif des Barreaux européens – Consultative Committee of European Bars.

26 E.g. for Austria: Standesrichtlinien, Art. 8.

27 E.g. Austria: Penal Code. Art. 146.

28 E.g. Switzerland Penal Code Art. 307; Germany: Bundesgerichtshof May 16, 1983, Monatschrift Deutsches Recht, 1983, 773.

29 E.g. Dutch Code of Civil Procedure, Art. 1065, para 1e.

30 The place of the seat of arbitration and not the place of the actual hearings (if different) is relevant.

8

The lawyer's duty to arbitrate in good faith*

(The 2001 Goff Lecture, published in Arbitration International, Vol. 18, No. 4, pp. 431-451 and re-published here by kind permission)

By V.V. Veeder
Barrister, Essex Court Chambers, United Kingdom
Council Member, ICC Institute of World Business Law

INTRODUCTION

It is a great honour to be asked to deliver this Goff lecture, not only because it is a privilege to follow in the footsteps of so many distinguished lecturers but also because this lecture bears the name of one of the most respected English jurists of my professional lifetime. There are many stories of Robert Goff: he was one of the greatest advocates I ever heard; he was a creative scholar; he was the most courteous judge; he is now a distinguished arbitrator; but above all else, he was and remains the epitome of fairness and human decency. To listen to his advocate's argument even in the most contentious case provoked no sense of ill-will, just despair at the power of his legal logic; and to lose a case before him as judge left only a strong sense of his intellectual honesty. To Lord Goff, the title of this lecture might seem so self-evident as to preclude any serious debate. Sadly, however, the debate is provoked by growing difficulties which cause the practice of transnational arbitration to fall short of his ideals.

---

* This text is a revised version of the author's 2001 Goff lecture delivered in Hong Kong on 5 December 2001 under the auspices of the City University of Hong Kong; and the editors acknowledge with thanks its permission to publish this article. The author is indebted to Mr Neil Hart for assistance in researching materials for this lecture. Any comments are welcome, which may be sent by email to vvveeder@compuserve.com. (The law and practice is here stated as at 1 December 2001.)

For the parties to an international commercial arbitration, justice should be the paramount objective; and procedural fairness by their legal representatives is subsumed in that single objective. But the practice of international arbitration is not so simple, certainly not for the parties' professional lawyers coming from different jurisdictions to a still different place of arbitration. Lawyers are not musicians or ballet dancers: a lawyer's training, skills and ethics are still essentially rooted in a national legal system; and it is far from clear how and to what extent national professional rules apply abroad to the transnational lawyer in the international arbitration process.

THE EUROPEAN UNION

For example, for a European Union lawyer practising abroad in a host Member State, Article 6 of the Directive 98/5/EC of 16 February 1998[1], which came into effect on 14 March 2000, prescribes rules of professional conduct in addition to the rules of that lawyer's home Member State: that lawyer is subject "to the same rules of professional conduct as lawyers practising under the relevant professional title of the host Member State in respect of all the activities he pursues in that territory". There is no further guidance in the Directive as to what professional rules of conduct apply to an English lawyer from London practising as an advocate in a Paris arbitration, except that the rules of the French avocat before a French court cannot simply be transposed to this English lawyer in an international arbitration[2].

Of course, an English lawyer working in the European Union's other Member States must also comply with the Code of Conduct for Lawyers in the European Union adopted in 1998 by the Conseil des Barreaux de l'Union Européenne (CCBE)[3]. The Code applies generally to the cross-border activities of any English lawyer working in the European Union and European Economic Area, including the great European arbitration centres of Paris, Geneva, Stockholm, Vienna, The Hague and Zurich. And the CCBE Code applies, at least in part, expressly to international arbitration[4].

Article 4.5, the 1998 Code provides that "the rules governing a lawyer's relations with the courts apply also to his relations with arbitrators". These particular rules are set out in Part 4 of the Code under Articles 4.1 to 4.4. Article 4.1 requires a lawyer who appears or takes part in a case before a Member States' court "to comply with the rules of conduct applied before that court". This rule is largely meaningless in the field of international arbitration because there are no "rules of conduct" applied generally to lawyers before an international arbitration tribunal. The major institutional rules of arbitration, including the ICC and LCIA Rules, are silent as to the conduct of a party's legal representative.

Articles 4.2 to 4.4 of the Code are more relevant to arbitration. Article 4.2 provides generally for the fair conduct of proceedings, excluding ex parte communications with the arbitrator and requiring settlement discussions not to be communicated to the arbitrator. Article 4.3 requires the lawyer to maintain due respect and courtesy towards the arbitrator; and Article 4.4 requires that "a lawyer shall never knowingly give false or misleading information to the court". These are valuable moral commandments; and this part of the Code is commendable for international practice. But that is the practical problem: it is such a small part that the Code provides no useful guidance on the most basic problems facing transnational practitioners of international commercial arbitration.

At best, of course, the Code applies only to regional practice for European Union lawyers in Western Europe. On a worldwide basis, what are the professional rules or guide for a lawyer seeking to discharge a duty to achieve procedural fairness in an international arbitration? The issue was raised ten years ago by a distinguished commentator, Jan Paulsson[5]; but his call went unheeded[6]. Yet the problem is real; the solution ought not to be insuperable; and the matter needs addressing by an international body because the problem applies generally to all of us, everywhere, practising as lawyers in the field of international arbitration. It applies especially in Hong Kong as a leading centre for international commercial arbitration, attracting legal practitioners from all over the world. To the question: what are the professional rules applicable to an Indian lawyer in a Hong Kong arbitration between a Bahraini claimant and a Japanese defendant represented by New York lawyers, the answer is no more obvious than it would be in London, Paris, Geneva and Stockholm. There is no clear answer; but perhaps, as we shall see, there should and could be.

PROCEDURAL UNFAIRNESS

In 1937, the ICC Congress met in Berlin, where its opening session was attended by the German Chancellor Hitler and his colleagues Goering and Goebbels. Even then, the ICC's new president, the American Thomas J Watson of IBM, felt able to proclaim the keynote of the conference: "world peace through world trade"[7]. Thomas Watson was right – but not as right as he would be 50 years later. The great cause today is the same but still greater: without world trade, there can be no world peace; international arbitration is the oil which lubricates the machinery of world trade; and the mechanics, the international arbitration practitioners, now deserve better practical guidance as to how to apply that oil. International commercial arbitration cannot wait another 50 years.

Let us start with the root of the problem: what is procedural unfairness? Many decades ago, when I was at school in Bristol, in the west of England, our school rugby team played a match against a local school badly endowed with playing fields. In fact, its rugby field lay on a steep hill; and given other demands for its use (which must have included abseiling), we had time for only one half of the match, all of which we played uphill – and lost, badly. In my ears, for a long time, the phrase "playing on a level playing field" resonated as the basic moral rule of fairness in any adversarial game. What was procedurally unfair, however, was not the pitch itself but the unfairness of playing uphill without the subsequent advantage of playing downhill. Given the range of geographic diversity, fairness is a general concept which must accommodate both flat and hilly ground.

The procedural difficulties in arbitration come from human rather than geographic diversity; and human diversity is surprisingly diverse. For example, there is a large house, beautifully built by one of our arbitration colleagues with a large circular drive leading to the main entrance, adjoining a magnificent tennis court. As many of you will know, the turning circle of a Rolls Royce is disappointingly large; and so it proved that the circular drive had to be enlarged – by taking out a large chunk of the tennis court. Tennis matches are still played at that house; the far half of the tennis court retained its full size although the near half is now severely truncated. The playing field is level, even if it is not equal; it is technically difficult serving and receiving a serve in a few feet of court; but it is not unfair if contestants take turns serving from the truncated half of the tennis court, which they apparently do. Where the tennis players are Rolls Royce owners, a turning circle is perhaps more important than a full tennis court; tennis can still be played fairly; and tennis teas can still be taken without tears. But what if not all players are Rolls Royce owners? Or if the field is not only uphill or unequal; but the other half is a cricket pitch, or a baseball diamond or a swimming pool – and there is no equivalent change at half time? Then there can be tears; and where the game is arbitration, it can raise acute questions of legal, professional and cultural diversity which are now potentially of immense importance in the practice of international arbitration by parties and particularly by their lawyers. Such diversity can unbalance the arbitral process.

This is different from the situation where both parties equally lack recourse to documentary production or factual testimony tested by cross-examination or the use of their own party-appointed expert witnesses. There is here a level and fair playing field; and of course awards have been enforced in a State court even if the arbitration's procedure was very different from the procedures employed in that court. We are also not dealing with deliberate dishonesty or criminal fraud here; and the international arbitral process can deal with acts of illegality[8], which thankfully seem to be rare. And we are not addressing non-criminal misconduct which is generally regarded as morally questionable; for example, the deliberate nomination of different specialist arbitrators in multiple disputes to deprive the other parties of specialist legal advice; or the deliberate conflicting out of specialist counsel by a party to the same end; or one party's beauty-parading of arbitral candidates which looks more at partiality than beauty; or the wilful aggravation of the parties' dispute in order to put unfair pressure on the adverse party.

We are concerned here with ambiguous acts short of deliberate dishonesty which cross the line of procedural fairness because no-one really knows quite where that line is now drawn at the international level. The issue can arise on challenges to awards under national legislation before State courts, including the UNCITRAL Model Law; and the enforcement of arbitration awards under the 1958 New York Convention. Then, however, it will often be too late to put right what was at the time, perhaps inadvertently, wrong.

The common starting point is necessarily the concept of procedural fairness; and whilst no arbitration tribunal can guarantee perfection at all times in deciding substantive law or fact (because judges and arbitrators are not deities), arbitrators can reasonably be asked always to deliver procedural fairness. In England, that objective is now recognized expressly in Lord Woolf's massive reforms to civil procedure in the State courts; for arbitration tribunals, independently, it is expressed by section 1(a) of the English Arbitration Act 1996[9]; and for both courts and arbitration tribunals, directly and indirectly, by the English Human Rights Act 1998 applying Article 6 of the European

Convention on Human Rights, guaranteeing a fair hearing to every person, legal and moral. But, as we all know, procedural fairness is no easy objective, and there is nothing "natural" about natural justice.

In the Anglo-Saxon adversarial system, fairness is dependent on the standards of conduct deployed by the parties and especially the parties' legal representatives, towards each other and towards the court or arbitration tribunal. As the US Supreme Court decided long ago in the Gideon case[10], a defendant's attorney at a criminal trial can be just as much an essential part of a properly constituted court as the judge or jury; and in complex civil litigation and arbitration, the same is almost invariably true. Judges just cannot do it as well or at all without the help of the parties' lawyers, and an international arbitration of any size would be equally incomplete without the parties' legal representatives. This symbiotic relationship can be readily illustrated with a recent cautionary tale from England.

THE CAUTIONARY TALE

In Vernon vs Bosley (No. 2) (1998)[11], the defendant nanny had killed by negligent driving two of the plaintiff's children and the plaintiff sued her for nervous shock. In a reserved judgement delivered long after the trial, the judge awarded damages for post-traumatic stress disorder based on expert evidence from a psychiatrist and psychologist; and the defendant then appealed to the Court of Appeal. The Court of Appeal heard this appeal and gave judgement up-holding liability but reducing the amount of damages. Before the formal order was drawn up, the defendant's counsel received anonymously through the post copies of a county court judgement in different family proceedings between the plaintiff and his divorced wife relating to the custody of their remaining children and of a judgement of the Court of Appeal (differently constituted) dismissing the plaintiff's appeal from that county court judgement.

What was significant was the expert issue in these family proceedings, taking place six months after the trial in the personal injury proceedings. In stark contrast to their evidence at that earlier trial, the same psychiatrist and psychologist had given expert evidence that the mental health of the plaintiff father had dramatically improved and that he was substantially, if not fully, recovered. This was not a case where these experts had given false evidence or expressed opinions which were incorrect; and in this sense neither had "changed his evidence", but rather only their prognosis as time had elapsed between the evidence in the personal injury trial and the later hearing in the family proceedings during which the plaintiff's mental health had significantly improved. As Lord Justice Stuart-Smith's judgement reports:

> "It appeared to the defendant's legal advisers [this must have been somewhat of an understatement] that this evidence was materially different from the picture presented to Sedley J [the trial judge] and this court [the Court of Appeal], and in particular it might affect the judge's findings as to the plaintiff's state of health at the time of the judgement and to the prognosis for the future. This would affect the level of general damages and also elements of future loss." (page 688D).

The plaintiff was morally blameless; he acted on the advice of his legal advisers. He was represented by different solicitors and counsel in the two sets of proceedings; and before the trial judge delivered his reserved judgement in the personal injury proceedings, his legal advisers advised him *not* to disclose the improved prognosis to the defendant, the trial judge or even later to the Court of Appeal; and when the plaintiff learnt that his former wife might disclose these medical reports obtained in the family proceedings to the defendant's insurers, his legal advisers sought and obtained from the High Court an injunction restraining her from doing so. Factually it is a complicated case; but what is clear was the absence of any dishonesty on the part of any of the plaintiff's legal advisers. They were plainly faced with an acute problem of professional ethics where their duty to the court appeared to conflict radically with the duty to their own client.

At the resumed hearing before the Court of Appeal, the defendant submitted that by one or more of three routes, discovery or disclosure of the later medical reports or the requirements not to mislead the court, the change in prognosis should have been made known by the plaintiff and his legal advisers. As to documentary discovery, by a majority, the Court of Appeal decided that the parties' duty continued up to judgement, after the conclusion of evidence and the trial; that the notes and medical reports were not privileged; and that these materials should have been disclosed to the defendant before the trial judge delivered his reserved judgement, even though both sides had long before closed their respective cases. As to the duty not to mislead the court, Lord Justice Stuart-Smith concluded:

> "I readily accept that the plaintiff's counsel did not deliberately intend to deceive the court and believed that the advice they gave [to the plaintiff] was sound. But in my judgement they made a serious error of judgement in failing to advise him on the need for disclosure. By an over-technical construction of the rules and a failure to appreciate that their previous conduct of the case would result in the court reaching an unjust result unless disclosure was made, they found themselves in an impossible position. By the time the case came to this court they should have appreciated that they could no longer seek to uphold the judge's judgement."

The defendant's second appeal was allowed by the Court of Appeal; and damages were further reduced. However, Lord Justice Evans dissented and would have dismissed the first part of this appeal and, whereas Lord Justice Stuart-Smith decided *(obiter)* that counsel's remedy was to resign if his advice to correct testimony or disclose documentation was rejected by his client, Lord Justice Thorpe decided that counsel's duty went much further: counsel had an overriding duty to disclose the relevant material to his opponent and, unless there was agreement between the parties otherwise, to the trial judge.

For present purposes, the point is simple. Difficult as this case was for the ethics of English lawyers before an English court, what would the answer be in a like case for a party's legal representatives acting in an international arbitration? For example, what would happen if a Hong Kong solicitor or counsel acting for an Australian party in an international arbitration in Singapore discovered weeks after the final hearing and as the tribunal was writing its final award, that part of their client's case was now quite wrong? Would these lawyers advise their client that a correction must be notified to their opponent and the tribunal? And if their client said "no", as it might and then dismissed them if they pressed their advice, would that counsel and solicitor have a duty to notify their foreign opponents or the arbitration tribunal abroad? The answer should probably be "yes" but juridically why? It is regrettable that these questions are currently beyond any clear answer, both in Hong Kong and elsewhere.

FOUR CHARACTERISTICS

International arbitration clearly raises more difficulties here than national practice before State courts; and there are four distinguishing characteristics which any solution needs to address.

First, as already discussed, practitioners in the field of international commercial arbitration extend over the full rainbow colours of human diversity around the world; the legal representatives of parties do not usually share the same national legal culture or practise subject to the rules of the same professional body. In the United Kingdom, long after the Act of Union with Scotland, it was on occasion still difficult for Scots and English lawyers to work with each other[12], but those difficulties pale into insignificance compared to the brave attempts within the European Union to subject the Member State's Bars and Law Societies to a uniform professional code of conduct, already mentioned above. Outside such legal regions, the problem is greater still. This does not mean that international practitioners are pirates sailing under no national flag; it means only that on the high seas, navigators need more than a coastal chart.

Secondly, unlike most national court systems, there is no appeal on the merits from an arbitration award. The need for finality generally outweighs justice in the particular case; and procedural mistakes can be left uncorrected even when caused by professional errors of judgement. In England, the 1996 Act has made an important difference in abolishing the English court's old power to remit an award to the arbitration tribunal on the grounds either that fresh evidence has become available after the award or that a procedural mishap has occurred short of any misconduct by the arbitration tribunal. These procedures can still be invoked in respect of appeals from English court judgements, but not any more in respect of English arbitration awards. A disgruntled losing party is left with the traditional but extreme remedy, if available, of challenging the award on the basis that it was obtained by fraud or contrary to public policy[13]. This quality of finality special to arbitration, but particularly so to international arbitration, means that it is even more important that an arbitration award should be the product of procedural fairness.

Thirdly, there is a lack of transparency in international arbitration. There are no useful statistics for institutional arbitration; and there are no reliable data at all for non-institutional or *ad hoc* arbitration. The whole activity takes place in a cloud of privacy without the same public scrutiny directed at State courts. In the absence of sufficient reported cases, it is not easy to learn how many arbitrations are unfairly conducted and, in particular, how fairness can be harmed by the conduct of parties' legal representatives. Yet the system of international arbitration does seem to work well. If so, like State litigation, the system must work because it is essentially self-policing – but self-policing by lawyers and arbitrators depends on practitioners having a clear idea of where the line is drawn between good and bad arbitration practices. If a lawyer advises a client that it must disclose voluntarily a relevant but harmful document or cannot plead fraud on existing materials, that client is entitled to know the reason why, and if there is no good reason, the pressures of international practice may mean that the client will find another lawyer who will do what the other has declined to do. In the field of international arbitration, like State litigation, there are many fish competing in the same sea. Clear rules and self-policing are an essential part of any solution.

Lastly, in arbitration, where the legal links between the parties usually derive from the contractual agreement to arbitrate (in whole or in part), the legal roots of a party's duty to play the game fairly must begin with that arbitration agreement, as a general contractual obligation to arbitrate in good faith. This is the most awkward characteristic: how can such a general obligation impose practical rules; and how does a contractual duty imposed on a party work itself through to rules influencing that party's legal representative? As to the former, it is obvious, even more so than in State litigation, that the rules need to be practical; and it is useless to maintain any rule at the level of supreme generality. A formulation based only on good faith could be too vague to be of practical use, and yet, in default of any other available legal principle, it is the necessary starting point. There is also a particular problem with a general principle of good faith as an English legal concept; in short, in recent history, it has not been very English at all.

GOOD FAITH

Good faith in the performance of civil procedural obligations is assumed by civilian lawyers. This duty of good faith is readily transposed from the duty of good faith in civil law. Professor Hanotiau, from Brussels, concluded in his work on multiparty arbitrations that it is a "basic principle of international commercial arbitration that the parties have the duty to co-operate in good faith in the performance of their agreement as well as in the arbitral proceedings", and another distinguished commentator from Greece, Antonias Dimolitsa, identified the source of that obligation: "the international principle of the inviolability of the arbitration agreement is actually just a special application of the principle of *pacta sunt servanda* which, together with the parallel application of good faith, is strictly applied to arbitration agreements"[14].

To an English lawyer, regrettably, the concept of good faith remains somewhat vague, and although the House of Lords has recently defined the term in the different context of a regulator's exemption from liability for the tort of misfeasance[15], English law on good faith says nothing about the activities of a party's legal representatives in an international arbitration. Former students of English law may recall that Professor Sir Roy Goode QC concluded in the first edition of his great work on commercial law[16] that, surprisingly, there was no general principle of English law that requires legal remedies to be exercised in good faith, adding that it was "at once the most remarkable and most reprehensible feature of English contract law". That was written even before the House of Lords decided in Walford vs Miles (1992)[17] that English law could not recognize and enforce obligations to negotiate "in good faith".

Nonetheless the contractual duty to arbitrate in good faith is recognized in the common law outside England. It is rare in international arbitration to see this duty spelt out, but there is a useful example in Hong Kong. In China Nanhai Oil vs Gee Tai Holdings (1994)[18], the Hong Kong High Court granted leave to enforce a CIETAC award on the ground that the losing defendant was estopped from relying on the improper constitution of the arbitration tribunal, which had been formed in Beijing and not Shenzhen as required by the parties' arbitration agreement. The facts need not concern us here, but Mr Justice Kaplan did not base his decision on the classic English equitable doctrine of estoppel. He cited the work on the New York Convention by the civilian Professor van den Berg, recognizing estoppel as a principle emanating from a party's general obligation to arbitrate in good faith "enshrined in the [New York] Convention's provisions". The learned Judge applied that duty of good faith so as to have required the defendant promptly to bring to the notice of the arbitration tribunal or CIETAC in Beijing its objections to the tribunal's formation, rather than wait two years after losing the arbitration before complaining for the first time that the arbitrators were chosen from the wrong CIETAC list of arbitrators.

What is needed is this kind of practical guidance on good faith for the legal representatives of parties. There is nothing to prevent that same approach being applied to the most contentious areas of professional practice: document production, the preparation of factual witness statements and the commissioning of independent expert reports. These procedures are now increasingly common in international arbitrations, given the widespread interest in the

International Bar Association's Rules on the Taking of Evidence in International Commercial Arbitration of June 1999, and the success of this initiative may answer the second part of the problem raised above, namely: how to influence the parties' lawyers.

THE IBA RULES

In 1983 there was a muted welcome for the first edition of these IBA Rules. Nonetheless, their quiet acceptance in practice over the next decade paved the way for the more ambitious second edition in 1999[19]. There was then criticism from some quarters over the new procedures for document production under Article 3 of the 1999 Rules – it either went too far in allowing a party to request unspecified documentation or not far enough in limiting that request to narrow and specific categories reasonably believed to exist. That criticism seems now to have died down. What was not at first controversial were Articles 4 and 5 dealing with factual witness statements and the written reports of party-appointed experts.

For international arbitration, the procedure whereby a party and not the tribunal leads its own factual and expert testimony is now well accepted by both civilian and common law practitioners and arbitrators, and it is the well-worn practice for a factual and expert-witness to reduce into writing in advance what would be their evidence-in-chief or direct examination, confining their oral testimony largely to cross-examination by the adverse party and the tribunal. This procedure removes the unfair element of surprise or deliberate ambush at the main hearing; it allows expert witnesses to meet and exchange views before the hearing (a procedure now reflected in Article 5(3) of the IBA Rules); and since hearing time is money, it saves both time and money by having everyone read these materials in advance of the main hearing without the need for direct testimony to be recited aloud. That is the theory, but as experience now shows, the practice can be different, and here experience has begun to mean bad experience.

There is an increasing tendency for a factual witness statement to take the form of special pleading prepared substantially by lawyers and not the witness (albeit later formally "approved" by that witness). This practice diminishes the statement's probative value and increases the need for oral cross-examination. There is again a similar practice whereby expert reports express less than independent expert opinions, again substantially prepared by lawyers and not the expert (albeit also "approved" by that expert); and this practice significantly complicates the task of the arbitration tribunal. As regards document production, there is increasing evidence that such production is assessed not by any uniform professional standards, but rather by subjective, client-driven rules calculated to support the factual and witness testimony to be adduced by that client.

THE PROBLEM IN PRACTICE

Why does any of this matter for international arbitration? It matters first because it can easily breed procedural unfairness in the particular case, and it matters generally because it attacks the integrity of the system of international arbitration. The system of self-policing may become impossible and there may be a gradual deterioration in the standards of legal professional conduct. The international arbitral process would then be brought into disrepute and, once its good reputation was lost, it could take decades to rebuild confidence[20]. To date, for example, the English court has rejected every attempt to attack a foreign award on strictly procedural grounds under the New York Convention. Indeed, there is still no reported case of an English court refusing enforcement of any foreign award on the ground of English public policy. However, there are now cases where the English court has broadened the public policy exception for English awards in section 68(2)(g) of the Arbitration Act 1996[21], and there is one recent case which illustrates that the English court may in future look critically at serious procedural unfairness under the same public policy exception in Article V(2)(b) of the New York Convention.

1. Document disclosure

The case related to documentary disclosure, allegedly made deficiently in the arbitration by the successful claimant. In Profilati Italia SRL vs Paine Webber Inc & anr (2001)[22], the losing applicant challenged the award on the grounds that part of it had been procured by the claimant in a way which was contrary to public policy under section 68 of the Arbitration Act 1996. The substance of its argument was that the claimant had wrongly failed to disclose two material documents which would have supported the applicant's case and, having failed to do so, that the claimant allowed its counsel to make submissions to the arbitration tribunal which could not have been made in the same way or with the same force if those documents had been disclosed and, to that extent, therefore, the award was improperly procured because the tribunal was effectively misled.

The English Commercial Court (Moore-Bick J) dismissed the application on its factual merits, but the judgement makes clear that, subject to factual proof, the application could be well founded under section 68(2)(g) of the 1996 Act. The learned Judge held:

> "17. It would be unwise in my view to attempt to define the circumstances in which an award might be set aside or remitted on public policy grounds, but in the light of that comment and of the language of subsection (2)(g) as a whole I think that where the successful party is said to have procured the award in a way which is contrary to public policy it will normally be necessary to satisfy the court that some form of reprehensible or unconscionable conduct on his part has contributed in a substantial way to obtaining an award in his favour."

And later:

> "19. Where an important document which ought to have been disclosed is deliberately withheld and as a result the party withholding it has obtained an award in his favour the court may well consider that he has procured that award in a manner contrary to public policy. After all, such conduct is not far removed from fraud."

Fraud is here actual dishonesty in the English legal sense. It is much more than a failure to disclose a document as a result of negligence or mishap or a simple error of judgement; but the Court acknowledged that something less than fraud might suffice if it qualified as "reprehensible or unconscionable conduct" – but what is that in an international commercial arbitration? It must presumably include "bad faith", even if that civilian term was never uttered by the English Court. If this analysis were correct, subject to further elaboration, the Court's approach could be readily imported into the IBA Rules on document production.

2. Factual witness statements and expert reports

For witness statements and expert reports, it is here again necessary for practical guidance to turn to court decisions because of the paucity of arbitration materials. It can be found in the English cases leading to the recent Woolf reforms.

■ Expert reports

The House of Lords held in Whitehouse vs Jordan (1987)[23] that even though some degree of consultation between experts and legal advisers was entirely proper, it was necessary that expert evidence presented to the court should be, and should be seen to be, the independent product of the expert, "uninfluenced as to form or content by the exigencies of litigation". In the Court of Appeal, which reversed the trial judge, Lord Denning MR had identified a number of flaws in a joint experts' report submitted by the plaintiff. Most prominent among these flaws was the intrusively editorial role played by the plaintiff's lawyers in preparing that evidence, as described by Lord Denning:

> In the first place, their joint report suffers to my mind from the way it was prepared. It was the result of long conferences between the two professors and counsel in London and it was actually "settled" by counsel. In short, it wears the colour of special pleading rather than an impartial report. Whenever counsel "settle" a document, we know how it goes. "We had better put this in". "We had better leave this out" and so forth. A striking instance is the way in which Professor Tizard's report was "doctored". The lawyers blacked out a couple of lines in which he agreed with Professor Strang [another expert-witness] that there was no negligence.

That counsel was a distinguished senior silk, of impeccable character and now an English High Court Judge. What he did was only what we all once did; it was a professional practice not only not wrong under the standards then prevailing in England; but not to do what he did could have been widely regarded at that time as professional negligence. Lord Denning's strictures changed that practice at the English Bar, almost overnight.

This new approach to expert evidence later formed part of Cresswell J's classic summary of the duties and responsibilities of expert witnesses in The Ikarian Reefer (1998)[24]. Foremost among those duties was the importance of the expert's autonomy from the influence of the parties to the litigation, as emphasized in Whitehouse. It required the expert-witness to provide "independent assistance to the Court by way of objective unbiased opinion in relation to matters within his expertise". That expert opinion must also be complete. Where there are conflicting experts' reports, the tribunal cannot reach any satisfactory finding if the relevant materials have been partially withheld by one or more expert witnesses. As Bracewell J held in Clough vs Tameside & Glossop HA (1998)[25]:

> "It is not for one party to keep their cards face down on the table so that the other party does not know the full extent of information supplied. Fairness dictates that a party should not be forced to meet a case pleaded or an expert opinion on the basis of documents he cannot see. Although civil litigation is adversarial, it is not permissible to withhold relevant information, or to delete or amend the contents of a report before disclosure."

The early identification and narrowing of expert issues is increasingly important in international commercial arbitration and, as already mentioned above, the practice of expert meetings is reflected in the IBA Rules. To make these procedures work fairly (and indeed to work at all), they must be played candidly, with open hands. As the English Court of Appeal noted in Naylor vs Preston Area Health Authority (1987)[26], the English courts:

> "have moved far and fast from a procedure where tactical considerations which did not have any relation to the achievement of justice were allowed to carry any weight. [W]hilst a party is entitled to privacy in seeking out the "cards" for his hand, once he has put his hand together, the litigation is to be conducted with all the cards face up on the table."

All this is a sea change from the former practice of lawyers in the English courts. It has all happened within the last 15 years without primary legislation until the Woolf reforms, being driven by English judges and practitioners.

■ Factual witness statements

The practice of taking factual witness statements requires urgent reform. Increasingly, many international arbitrators pay little credence to written witness statements on any contentious issue, unless independently corroborated by other reliable evidence. It is perhaps surprising that many sophisticated practitioners have not yet understood that their massive efforts at reshaping the testimony of their client's factual witnesses is not only ineffective but often counter-productive. Most arbitrators have been or remain practitioners; and they can usually detect the "wood-shedding" of a witness[26]. In England, there is a recent case where wood-shedding was taken to an extreme.

In Aquarius Financial Enterprises vs Lloyds' Underwriters (2001),(28) where the English Commercial Court was concerned with a vessel allegedly destroyed deliberately by fire, Toulson J. held that it was the English solicitor's duty to ensure that any factual witness was interviewed by the solicitor himself, or if that was not practicable, by a person who could be relied upon to exercise the same standard as an English solicitor. This decision was provoked by the treatment of a particular witness, Mr Schoenig, who was on board the vessel when the fire broke out; and the interviewer was Mr Ashton, a marine surveyor and investigator, previously a police officer and (more significantly) for many years a CID officer attached to the anti-terrorist squad. In cross-examination, Mr Ashton had explained his interviewing technique as follows:

- **Q.** You resorted to intimidation to obtain the evidence you wanted?
  A. I don't call it intimidation, I was forceful. I was dealing with a person that I thought was lying to me; I was not going to pussyfoot around. I knew the type of person I was dealing with. This was a very street-wise person.

- **Q.** You had formed the conclusion that this man was not going to give you the evidence that you needed unless you bullied him, so you set about bullying him?
  A. I had not formed that conclusion. I formed that conclusion at the end when he didn't give me the evidence that he could have given me. I didn't set out to bully him, I set out to talk to him in a nice manner and to deal with the matter as I would with any other witness. It was his attitude that made me become forceful and angry at times.

The learned Judge commented adversely on this style of interrogation. He said:

> "43. In English litigation, civil or criminal, there can be no proper place for trying to persuade a potential fact witness what he should say, let alone by bullying, threat or inducements[29]. Such methods are totally unacceptable. Mr Ashton's conviction that Mr Schoenig was lying is no conceivable justification. If Mr Ashton had succeeded, and if Mr Delettrez [another witness] had not been recording the conversation, the result would have been a [written witness] statement from Mr Schoenig which could have been put in evidence under the Civil Evidence Act without either the court or the opposing party knowing how it had been obtained."

The learned Judge then referred to the procedure by which witness statements ordinarily stand as witnesses evidence in chief, an integral part of practice in the English Commercial Court for some years but now prescribed under Rule 32.5(2) of the Civil Procedure Rules. He then cited Part H1.3 of the Commercial

Court Guide, which provides that: "whilst it is recognised that in commercial cases, a witness statement will usually be prepared by legal representatives, the witness statement must, so far as practicable be in the witness's own words". His judgement continued:

> "46. It cannot be too strongly emphasised that this means the words which the witness wants to use and not the words which the person taking the statement would like him to use.
>
> 47. Part H1.4 of the Commercial Court Guide provides that the rules of any professional body regarding the drafting of witness statements must also be observed.
>
> 48. The Law Society's Guide to the Professional Conduct of Solicitors provides guidance on the taking of witness statements. It requires a high degree of skill and professional integrity. The object is to elicit that which the witness is truthfully able to say about relevant matters from his or her own knowledge or recollection, uninfluenced by what the statement taker would like him or her to say.
>
> 49. Counsel on both sides expressed anxiety that this is in practice not what generally happens even when statements are taken by solicitors. If it is not, the situation is worrying. In the USA pre-trial depositions of witnesses are a standard feature of civil litigation[30]. The process is costly and time-consuming. Our system is quicker and cheaper, but it depends for its proper working on witness statements being properly taken. Bad practices, like bad money, tend to drive out good. If bad practices in the taking of witness statements come to be seen as normal, so that witness statements become lawyers' artefacts rather than the witnesses' words, their use will have to be reconsidered. Central to the problem is the ignorance of the court and the other party about how any witness statement has in fact been taken. It might therefore be thought salutary that there should be a written declaration by the person who prepared the statement giving information about how, when and where it was prepared and certifying compliance with any appropriate code of practice.
>
> 50. Moreover where parties are represented in litigation by solicitors (as is almost invariably the case in the Commercial Court), I would regard it as part of their duty to ensure, so far as lies within their power, that any witness statements taken after they have been instructed are taken either by themselves or, if for some reason that is not practicable, by somebody who

can be relied upon to exercise the same standard as should apply if the statements were taken by the solicitors themselves."

It would be a foolish English practitioner who did not now take heed of the strictures in this judgement.

THE WOOLF REFORMS

The Woolf reforms have accelerated but did not initiate these judicial reforms in the English courts. All these reforms have undoubtedly made English practice easier by setting out more clearly the rules for English lawyers to follow, particularly in the preparation of factual witness statements and expert reports[31]. The cardinal principle requires the draft witness statement to reflect accurately the witness' evidence[32], and the Commercial Court Guide expressly warns that: "great care should be exercised when excluding any material which is thought to be unhelpful to the party calling the witness and no material should be excluded which might render the statement anything other than the truth, the whole truth and nothing but the truth". Expert witnesses must certify that they understand their duty to the court, as set out in Appendix 12 to the Guide (which derives substantially from Cresswell J's judgement in The Ikarian Reefer), and experts must address their reports to the court. It is the express duty of experts to help the court on the matters within their expertise (CPR 35.3(1)). This duty is paramount and overrides any obligation to the person from whom an expert has received instructions or by whom he or she is paid (CPR 35.3(2)).

This Appendix 12 lists specific rules:

1 Expert evidence presented to the Court should be, and should be seen to be, the independent product of the expert uninfluenced by the exigencies of litigation.

2 An expert-witness should provide independent assistance to the Court by way of objective unbiased opinion in relation to matters within his expertise. An expert-witness should never assume the role of an advocate.

3 An expert-witness should not omit to consider material facts which could detract from his concluded opinion.

4 An expert-witness should make it clear when a particular question or issue falls outside his expertise.

5 If an expert's opinion is not properly researched because he considers that

insufficient data is available, then this must be stated with an indication that the opinion is no more than a provisional one.

6 In a case where an expert-witness who has prepared a report could not assert that the report contained the truth, the whole truth and nothing but the truth without some qualification, that qualification should be stated in the report.

7 If, after exchange of reports, an expert-witness changes his view on a material matter having read another expert's report or for any other reason, such change of view should be communicated in writing (through legal representatives) to the other side without delay, and when appropriate to the Court.

The expert-witness must certify that he or she has read and understood Appendix 12 and that he or she has complied and will continue to comply with its terms at all stages of involvement in the case. The expert must also certify that the assumptions on which his or her opinion are based are not unreasonable or unlikely or that if they are, the expert has said so; the expert must certify that the facts stated in his or her report within his or her own knowledge have been identified as such and are true; the expert must certify that the opinions expressed in the report represent his or her true professional opinion; and the expert must of course sign the opinion so as to make it his or her own expert opinion. This is all very uncontroversial; it works in practice for the English Commercial Court and suitably adapted it could work equally for international commercial arbitration.

POSSIBLE SOLUTIONS

The question first arises whether international arbitration is susceptible to reform at all. From the English perspective, the answer is easy: if Lord Woolf could so massively reform English civil procedure, then nothing is beyond reform anywhere. For international commercial arbitration, such reforms must be possible; but equally these cannot be achieved by a mono-cultural approach, and, as indicated above, there are also certain criteria for any possible solutions. The initiative lies in the hands of international arbitrators and practitioners and, if ignored for much longer, it may pass to state or regional regulators with less affection for the arbitration process.

The general contractual duty of good faith can provide the legal umbrella for both civilian and common law lawyers, but by itself the doctrine is too general to provide an effective practical guide for parties' lawyers practising in the field of international arbitration. Also, that guide cannot be a national or regional code of conduct, crudely transplanted to apply to transnational lawyers arbitrating in that country or applied to its own national lawyers practising in another host State. Equally, it cannot be a guide designed to govern a lawyer's relations with a State court. International arbitration is different from State and national practice: it is *sui generis*, and, in its different forms, it is a much more varied and flexible procedure which requires its own guide. Nonetheless, despite its practitioners' legal and cultural differences, the practice of international arbitration is increasingly subject to harmonization. It is becoming supra national and the solution could also be supra national. We saw this with the 1986 IBA Code of Ethics for International Arbitrators[33], and we see it with the 1999 IBA Rules of Evidence. Like these IBA Rules, what is needed is a voluntary solution – a guide rather than a model law or disciplinary code – and the best way to start is with micro-solutions, rather than a grand project where the usual difficulties could hinder progress for a long time, even then leading perhaps only to moralistic and impractical solutions[34]. If the first step is the hardest, however long the eventual journey, let us make it small and easy.

For witness statements under the 1999 IBA Rules, taking the suggestion proposed in the Aquarius case, let there be appended to the witness statement a written declaration by the parties' legal representative who procured the statement giving his or her name and professional qualification, and giving information about how, when and where the statement was prepared, including a statement of time spent by witness and representative respectively. For expert reports under the 1999 IBA Rules, taking the success of the Woolf reforms, let there be a similar declaration by the party's legal representative, together with a statement by the expert-witness acknowledging his or her independent duty along the lines of the Woolf requirements, listed above. For document production, international arbitrators should more readily complain at a party's delinquent conduct, to the extent of drawing expressly an adverse inference on the merits from procedural delinquency or making a special order on costs.

These are modest suggestions; and others will wish to add their own suggestions derived from their own experience. Once collated by the IBA or another international organization, they could make a difference in improving best practice. Bad practices, like bad money, do tend to drive out good. If bad practices in the taking of written witness statements or commissioning independent expert reports come to be seen as normal by users and by international arbitrators, their probative value will be diminished still further; and their use will have to be reconsidered. As for deficient documentary production, cynicism will breed contempt for the arbitral process. None of this is a cry of despair. On the contrary, it is a measure of the ever-increasing success of international arbitration that it must meet new challenges and provide new practical solutions on a larger scale. If, as has been said, international arbitration is the only show in town for international trade, let it at least not be a tennis game played with half the court always missing or a rugby match played by lawyers, like Sisyphus, eternally uphill.

Appendix

An old ethical Code (to be adapted)

Gilbert and Sullivan's "Iolanthe" was first performed at the Savoy Theatre on 25 November 1882 and the libretto contains in Act One a possible starting point in the distant future for an ethical code for international arbitration practitioners, substituting international arbitration for the English Bar, etc. It is the song of the Lord Chancellor of England and Wales, who (as he sang in Arcadia) always kept his duty strictly before his eyes, and it was to that fact (he sang) that he owed advancement to his distinguished position:

When I went to the Bar as a very young man,
(Said I to myself, said I),
I'll work on a new and original plan,
(Said I to myself, said I),
I'll never assume that a rogue or a thief
Is a gentleman worthy of implicit belief,
Because his attorney has sent me a brief,
(Said I to myself, said I).
Ere I go into court I will read my brief through
(Said I to myself, said I),
And I'll never take work I'm unable to do
(Said I to myself, said I),
My learned profession I'll never disgrace
By taking a fee with a grin on my face,
When I haven't been there to attend to the case
(Said I to myself, said I).
I'll never throw dust in a juryman's eyes
(Said I to myself, said I),
Or hoodwink a judge who is not over-wise
(Said I to myself, said I),
Or assume that the witnesses summoned in force
In Exchequer, Queen's Bench, Common Pleas, or Divorce,
Have perjured themselves as a matter of course
(Said I to myself, said I).
In other professions in which men engage
(Said I to myself, said I),
The Army, the Navy, the Church, and the Stage
(Said I to myself, said I),
Professional licence, if carried too far,
Your chance of promotion will certainly mar-
And I fancy the rule might apply to the Bar
(Said I to myself, said I!).

END NOTES

1 Directive 98/5/EC of the European Parliament and of the Council of 16 February 1998 to facilitate practise of the profession of lawyer on a permanent basis in a Member State other than that in which the qualification was obtained. OJ L 077, 14/03/1998 0036-0043.

2 See Société International Contractors Group c/ Me X (1992) Rev. de l'Arb 609 (where the Paris Cour d'appel decided that the prohibition against pacta de quota litis for a French avocat in French court proceedings was inapplicable to an avocat representing an Italian party to an international arbitration held in Paris under the ICC Rules; see commentaries by Leboulanger, ibid 615, and Paulsson, infra.

3 Code of Conduct for Lawyers in the European Union adopted by the 18 national delegations representing the Bars and Law Societies of the European Union at the Conseil des Barreaux de l'Union Européenne (CCBE) Plenary session held in Lyons on 28 November 1998. Copies are available from the CCBE website <http://www.ccbe.org>. (The 1998 Code originated with the Perugia Declaration made by the Bars and Law Societies of the European Community on 16 September 1977. It dealt with a lawyer's social function, integrity, confidentiality, independence, professional spirit and publicity, and it updates the 1988 Code.)

4 By Paragraph 1.5 of the CCBE Code, it applies to "the cross-border activities of the lawyer within the EU and EEA. Cross-border activities shall mean: (a) all professional contacts with lawyers of Member States other than their own; and (b) the professional activities of the lawyer in a Member State other than his own, whether or not the lawyer is physically present in that Member State." Its terms are wide enough to apply to lawyer-arbitrators as well as a party's legal representative.

5 Paulsson, "Standards of Conduct for Counsel in International Arbitration" in (1992) 3 Amer. Rev. Int. Arb. 214, where the author analysed the earlier 1988 CCBE Code of Conduct.

6 Indeed, many years ago, the arbitration conference in Brussels at which we were both to deliver papers on this subject was cancelled by the organizers, the Chartered Institute of Arbitrators, apparently for lack of interest.

7 Ridgeway, Merchants of Peace (1938) at p. 384.

8 For example, see Roth, "False Testimony at International Arbitration Hearings Conducted in England and Switzerland – A Comparative View" in (1994) 11 J. Int'l Arb. 5.

9 Section 1(a) of the 1996 Act states as a principle on which Part I of the Act is founded: "the object of arbitration is to obtain the fair resolution of disputes by an impartial tribunal without unnecessary delay or expense".

10 Gideon vs Wainwright 372 US 335 (1963).

11 Vernon vs Bosley (No 2)(1999) QB 18 (Stuart-Smith and Thorpe LJJ, Evans LJ dissenting; see also Vernon vs Bosley (No. 1)(1997) 1 All ER 577.

12 See D.L. Carey-Miller, "The Advocate's Duty to Justice" in (1981) 97 LQR 127.

13 Section 68(2)(g) of the 1996 Act: see Mustill & Boyd's 2001 Companion (2001) at pp. 352-354, to which we return below.

14 Hanotiau, "Complex Multicontract-Multiparty Arbitration" in (1998) Arbitration International 369; Dimolitsa, '"Arbitration Agreements and Foreign Investments: The Greek State" in (1988) 5 J. Int'l Arb. 17 at p. 39.

15 See Three Rivers District Council vs Governor and Company of the Bank of England (No 3)[2000] 2 WLR 1220 for the first judgement; and for the second judgement, see [2001] 2 All ER 513. (Section 29 of the Arbitration Act 1996 exempts, in similar terms, an arbitrator from liability save for "bad faith").

16 Goode, Commercial Law (1982, 1st ed.) at p. 117.

17 Walford vs Miles (1992) 2 A.C. 128. This decision has generated a mass of comment, conveniently summarized in Beatson and Friedman (eds), Good Faith and Fault in Contractual Law (1995) at pp. 36-42. See also Brownsford et al. (ed), Good Faith in Contract (1998, Ashgate).

18 China Nanhai Oil Joint Services Corporation vs Gee Tai Holdings Limited (1995) XX ICCA Yearbook 671 (reporting the Decision dated 13 July 1994 of the Hong Kong High Court (Kaplan J), citing van den Berg, The New York Convention (1981) at p. 185).

19 IBA Rules on the Taking of Evidence in International Commercial Arbitration, adopted by a resolution of the IBA Council on 1 June 1999, available on <www.ibanet.org>.

20 There is an existing analogy with the loss of professional courtesy between English arbitration practitioners, once the norm and now increasingly the exception. As Lord Mustill warned a decade ago: "There is precious little self-discipline, comradeship or community spirit between the parties to a typical arbitration" (1992) 9 J. Int'l Arb. 5 at p. 15. There is no rational explanation for this regrettable change, which is particularly evident in correspondence, but

the process now seems irreversible.

21 Section 68 of the 1996 Act provides: "(1) A party to arbitral proceedings may apply to the court challenging an award in the proceedings on the ground of serious irregularity affecting the tribunal, the proceedings or the award. (2) Serious irregularity means an irregularity of one or more of the following kinds which the court considers has caused or will cause substantial injustice to the applicant. (g) the award being obtained by fraud or the award or the way in which it was procured being contrary to public policy."

22 Profilati Italia SRL vs Paine Webber Inc & anr(2001) 1 Lloyd's Rep. 715.

23 Whitehouse vs Jordan (1987) 1 WLR 246.

24 The Ikarian Reefer (1993) 2 Lloyd's Rep. 68 at pp. 81-82. The Court of Appeal reversed the judgement but approved this passage intact: see (1995) 1 Lloyd's Rep. 455 at p. 496.

25 Clough vs Tameside & Glossop HA (1998) 1 WLR 1478 at p. 1484.

26 Naylor vs Preston Area HA (1987) 1 WLR 958 at p. 967.

27 In one case, where a witness had been thoroughly coached by his party's lawyers in successive dress rehearsals before a "shadow" arbitration tribunal, the witness concluded his testimony before the actual tribunal by congratulating, inadvertently, the opposing counsel for the brevity of his cross-examination, on the ground that it was "the shortest of all".

28 Aquarius Financial Enterprises Inc & Bernard Deletirez vs Certain Underwriters at Lloyd's (2001) 2 Lloyd's Rep. 542.

29 See also Odyssey Re London Limited vs OIR Run-Off Limited (unreported; The Times Law Report, 13 March 2000; Nourse, Brooke & Buxton LJJ, latter dissenting) a case where the perjured evidence of a director was treated as that of a company obtaining a judgement which was on that ground set aside, where Brooke LJ severely deprecated the "charm-offensive" deployed by the company's English solicitors towards the alleged perjurer.

30 Outside the USA, witness depositions are not usual in international commercial arbitration. Although depositions can remove much of the need for direct and cross-examination of witnesses, the procedure takes place away from the arbitration tribunal (who cannot therefore make their own assessment of the witness); it does not always save time and expense; and the practice is regarded by the English courts as inconsistent with both court and arbitration procedures: see Commerce and Industry Insurance Co of Canada vs Lloyd's Underwriters (2002) 1 Lloyd's Rep. 219; and Refco Capital Markets vs Crédit Suisse (First Boston)(2001) EWCA CIV 1733 (Court of Appeal; 21 November

2001; unreported).

31 Part H1 of the Commercial Court Guide and CPR Part 32 and 32PD, paragraphs 17 to 25. For English solicitors, there is general guidance in Chapter 21 of their Code of Conduct Rules; and as officers of the court, solicitors bear a general but wide-ranging duty not to mislead the court. The English Bar can now take and assist in taking a witness statement in civil cases; and the rules are set out in Paragraph 704-5 of the Bar's Code of Conduct and an approved guide, "Guidance on the Preparation of Witness Statements".

32 As to the contents of an expert report, the relevant rules are set out in Part 35 of the Civil Procedural Rules 1998 and its Practice Direction, together with Section H2 and Appendix 12 of the Commercial Court Guide. There is an Expert-Witness Protocol (Version 1.0) prepared by the Official Referees Solicitors Association (ORSA) for use in the Technology and Construction Court (available at <www.courtservice.gov.uk/notices/tcc/tcc-tecsa-ewp.htm>), and there is also a draft Code of Guidance for Experts of September 1999 awaiting approval as a Practice Direction. (These documents will be revised in 2002.)

33 See Branson, "Ethics for International Arbitrators" in (1987) 3 Arbitration International 72.

34 The English Bar developed for centuries without any formal code of conduct until very recently, although a useful code was expressed informally by the Lord Chancellor in Iolanthe (see appendix), which speaks for itself.

Concluding remarks

By Laurent Lévy
Co-Editor
Attorney-at-Law, Partner, Schellenberg Wittmer, Geneva, Switzerland
Council Member, ICC Institute of World Business Law

The papers collected in this volume are an illustration of the freedom the arbitrators enjoy in shaping "their" procedure, subject to other arrangements between the parties. There is no international code of arbitration procedure to limit the discretion of the arbitrators:

> "It should be underlined that procedural public policy will constitute only a simple exclusion provision, namely that it will merely have a protective function and will not generate any positive rules. This is because the legislature did not desire that procedural public policy should be extensively interpreted and that there should arise a code of arbitral procedure to which the procedure, as freely selected by the parties, should be subjected"[1].

Besides the parties' consent, there is only one mandatory limit to the arbitrators' discretion in procedural matters, namely the hard core of procedural public policy restricted to the "equal treatment of the parties" and "due process". As Article 18 of UNCITRAL Model Law expresses it: "*The parties shall be treated with equality and each party shall be given a full opportunity of presenting its case*"[2].

Beyond the requirements of procedural public policy, where do the arbitrators find their guidelines to establish their procedural rules?

The contributions to this volume show that two principles are generally accepted, although not necessarily resulting from the procedural *ordre public*.

First, the arbitrators should have a personal knowledge of the evidence. Subject to an agreement of the parties to the contrary (for instance for the deposition of a witness), the arbitrators should attend the taking of oral evidence. Otherwise, the arbitrators would not fully discharge their duties and possibly commit a serious irregularity. However, the discretion of the arbitrators in the taking of evidence is such that courts will not necessarily quash an award because a truncated tribunal or the chairman alone presided over the taking of oral evidence[3].

Second, the arbitrators have full power to assess evidence adduced before them and, in principle no court will review the weighing of evidence, be it upon a challenge or the enforcement of the award. There are no strict rules of evidence limiting the admissibility of any oral evidence. Anyone can be a witness, including a party in its own case. Any form of oral evidence is permitted, whether in the form of a deposition, a testimony, a video conference, witness conferencing, a telephone conference or any other. The arbitrators will simply weigh the evidence in question.

Beyond the rules of procedural public policy and these two generally accepted principles, the reports in this volume show that arbitrators will avoid any references to national laws of procedure, including the procedural laws in use before the courts at the seat of arbitration, and will primarily seek efficiency, predictability and transparency.

Efficiency means reaching as early as possible an enforceable and satisfactory determination of the case, saving as much as possible on the unavoidable expenses.

Predictability requires the arbitrators to evaluate the expectations of the parties and to address as soon as possible the procedural issues likely to arise during the course of the arbitration and no others: the ICC system offers an opportunity to determine at the outset such procedural issues in a meeting with the parties on the occasion of the execution of the terms of reference.

Transparency is also well served by this early discussion of the procedural rules and the arbitrators may want to take advantage of the adoption of the provisional timetable to convey their messages to the parties and sense their reactions to their various proposals.

It is thus for the arbitrators to decide how they will let each party fully exercise its right to put its case. Guided by considerations of time efficiency, limitation of costs and otherwise available evidence, the arbitrators will decide whether to order, refuse or restrict oral evidence and how to organise it.

It seems that the arbitration community does recognise these principles and, one way or another, the papers in this volume do refer to them.

One corollary is that there is no real procedural custom: each arbitrator will tailor the individual arbitration proceedings to his liking, taking into consideration the peculiarities of the case. Each practised arbitrator possesses a standard form of "constitution order and applicable procedural rules" which he will adjust to the needs of the specific proceedings.

The flexibility of arbitration explains why detailed procedural rules and guidelines failed to obtain great success[4]. This also explains why the IBA Rules of Evidence seem most successful as guidelines and less frequently govern per se an arbitration.

Four examples will evidence this flexibility in international practice:

- Is an oral hearing compulsory?
- Is it mandatory for the arbitrators to hear witnesses?
- What about witness statements? Is there a tendency to consider the witness statements as the direct examination of the witness? What is the value of the witness statement if the witness fails to appear for oral examination?
- Is there a general usage as to expert oral evidence?

There is no general answer. This apparent lack of uniformity will of course not mean that some principles should not be generally accepted.

For instance, there is consensus in the arbitration world that counsel may "prepare" the witnesses for a hearing and assist them in preparing their witness statements: everyone seems to agree that witness statements will be a factor of efficiency (especially if counsel see to it that such documents focus on facts relevant and material to the issues at bar) and may reduce the length and costs of the evidentiary hearing. The parties should be aware of the "rules of the game" and not expect a witness to come unprepared to a hearing. Nevertheless, faced with parties from different parts of the world, especially if counsel appear somewhat inexperienced, the arbitrators may feel the need to make their own requirements more specific, for instance in letting the parties know how much coaching they would consider acceptable. They will be "in full charge of the hearings" (Article 21.3 ICC Rules) and should thus leave as few ambiguities as possible about their expectations. It is telling that, in his paper, as an experienced arbitration practitioner as Robert Rifkind referred to the preparation of witnesses by counsel "in America"[5].

It thus appears that oral evidence in arbitration is both particular and common.

It is particular because it is different from the taking of evidence in front of any State jurisdiction: the arbitrators can (in principle) not order the hearing of witnesses under penalties of law, will (in principle) not swear in witnesses. False testimonies in front of arbitrators are normally not an offence[6]. It is admissible to hear any witnesses: as arbitration disputes arise most of the times out of the performance of a contract, there are few truly independent witnesses. In other words, there are no standard rules as to how to weigh the evidence. The arbitrators will have to rely on their own experience and wisdom to forge their conviction.

Oral evidence in arbitration is, however, common because the same principles will apply to documentary evidence.Truly, the arbitral tribunal could not decide to conduct the proceedings on the basis of oral evidence and exclude documentary evidence. This is a difference between oral and documentary evidence as to their admissibility. However, beyond this issue of admissibility, there is no real difference between oral and documentary evidence.

In both instances, there are no limitations to the power of the arbitrators to assess the evidence. There is no peculiar sanctity of some documents (deeds, notarized documents, affidavits under oath) and there is no rule restricting evidence to the use of documentary evidence.

As a practical matter, the use of a forged document in an arbitration will have the same consequences as the use of a false testimony. The arbitrators will not report the occurrence to the criminal justice. They will disregard the tainted evidence and probably draw some inference as to the credibility of the party.

There seem to be two reasons to this fading of the dividing line between evidence in writing and oral evidence in arbitration.

Due to the evolution of the technology, the differences between documents and testimonies tend to disappear. The proverb *"verba volant scripta manent"* is losing most of its significance. DVDs, CDs and magnetic tapes will keep oral statements. A voice recognition device will make an oral statement look like a typed document. Moreover, e-mail and SMS messages are drafted as they would be spoken rather than as a formal document. There is an overlap of the two types of evidence, namely witness statements which are a document but part of oral evidence.

Arbitration practice shows the emergence of another distinction, namely between contemporaneous evidence and evidence prepared with a view to the arbitration.

The arbitrators have a tendency to rely more confidently on the former, especially on the contractual documentation, the correspondence between the parties and, to a certain extent, internal memoranda and site visits (precisely if the site still permits to ascertain its original condition).

This volume is a tribute to the trust in international arbitrators: party autonomy will vest them with the widest discretion to hear oral evidence, subject always to keeping the parties equal and hearing their respective cases. The parties entrust the arbitrators with resolving their dispute for them because they are unable to find a solution on their own: they thus agree that the arbitrators will be made privy to the history of the case, as they know it themselves, and that the arbitrators have all the necessary powers, for instance the discretion to hear any witness "they control" and, possibly, others. They expect to remain active in this process, so that the arbitrators should always endeavour to seek their (or their counsel's) full joint cooperation in the procedural matters in spite of their confrontation on the merits. The savvy arbitrator will use sparingly of his power, keep the parties informed of his policies, in a word will remember that *"On gouverne mal quand on gouverne trop. Un homme qui traite avec un autre homme, doit être attentif et sage; il doit veiller à son intérêt, prendre les informations convenables, et ne pas négliger ce qui est utile"*[7]. The necessary, all the necessary but not more than the necessary and always with the full knowledge of the parties.

END NOTES

1 Swiss Federal Tribunal, 30 December 1994, F. and U. v. W., Bulletin ASA 1994, 217, 221. Comp. A. Baum in Liber Amicorum, K.H. Böckstiegel (C. Heymanns, 2001), p. 21 passim.

2 Cf. Art. 33 (1996) English Arbitration Act. Compare with Article 33 1996 English Arbitration Act, Article 182.3 Swiss PILA.

3 See Paris Court of Appeal 12.87, 13 March 1987, cited by Sophie Crépin, Les sentences arbitrales devant le juge français, LGDJ, Paris 1995, fn. 4 ad. No. 419 p. 261.

4 For instance, the UNCITRAL "Guidelines for preparatory conferences in arbitral proceedings"; see P. Lalive, De la fureur réglementaire, 1994, Bulletin ASA, p. 213.

5 If this hint is not sufficiently clear, the reader may want to refer to the first paragraph of Mr Rifkind's presentation.

6 For the exceptions to such principles, see above A. Dimolitsa, ad. pp. 24-36.

7 Discours préliminaire du premier projet de code civil français in Conférence du code civil, Firmin Didot, Paris, An XII 1805, p.lxviii.

Selected bibliography

A. ORAL EVIDENCE

BAGNER (HANS)

"Need for Rules of Evidence in International Arbitration", 25 Int'l Bus. Law. 175 (1997)

BAKSHI (P.M.)

"Arbitration Law and Evidentiary Aspects", 1987(2) Company L.J. 63

BARCLAY (CEDRIC)

"Harmonisation of Evidence", in ICCA, Fifth Int'l Arb'n Congress: Proceedings C IIB 1-4 (1975)

BAUM (AXEL H.)

"Reconciling Anglo-Saxon and Civil Law Procedure: The Path to a Procedural Lex Arbitrations", in Law of International Business and Dispute Settlement in the 21st Century: Liber Amicorum Karl-Heinz Böckstiegel 21 (R. Briner, L.Y. Fortier, K.P. Berger & J. Bredow, eds, 2001)

BLESSING (MARC)

The ICC Arbitration Process. Part III: The Procedure Before the Arbitral Tribunal, 3 ICC Court Arb. Bull. 19 (No. 2, 1992)

BÖCKSTIEGEL (KARL-HEINZ)

Presenting Evidence in International Arbitration, 16 ICSID Rev. – Foreign Investment L.J. 1 (2001)

Beweiserhebung in internationalen Schiedsverfahren (Cologne 2001)

DE BOISSÉSON (MATTHIEU)

Introduction comparative aux systémes d'administration des preuves dans les pays de common law et des pays de tradition romaniste/Comparative Introduction to the System of Producing Evidence in Common, Law Countries and Countries of Roman Law Tradition, in ICC, Taking of Evidence in International Arbitral Proceedings 85 (1990)

CECCON (ROBERTO)

"UNCITRAL Notes on Organizing Arbitral Proceedings and the Conduct of Evidence", 14 J. Int'l Arb. 68 (No. 2, 1997)

DELVOLVÉ (JEAN-LOUIS)

"Practices for Presenting Evidence in International Commercial Arbitration", in ICCA, 5th Int'l Arb'n Congress: Proceedings C IIc 1-10 (1975)

DIERYCK (CHRISTIAN)

"Procédure et moyens de preuve dans l'arbitrage commercial international", [1986] 7 Int'l Arb. Gazette 227

"Procédure et moyens de preuve dans l'arbitrage commerical international", 1988 Rev. Arb. 267

EIJSVOOGEL, P., ED.

Evidence in International Arbitration Proceedings (London 1994)

ELSING (SIEGFRIED H.) & (JOHN M.)

"Townsend, Bridging the Common Law-Civil Law Divide in Arbitration", 18 Arb. Int'l 59 (2002)

FISCHER-ZERMIN (VINCENT) & JUNKER (ABBO)

"Between Scylla and Charybdis: Fact Gathering in German Arbitration", 4 J. Int'l Arb. 9 (No. 2, 1987)

FRIEDLAND (PAUL D.)

"Combining Civil Law and Common Law Elements in the Presentation of Evidence in International Commercial Arbitration", 12 Mealey's Int'l Arb. Rep. 25 (No. 9, 1997)

"A Standard Procedure for Presenting Evidence in International Arbitration", 11 Mealey's Int'l Arb. Rep. 25 (No. 4, 1996)

GRIFFIN (PETER R.)

"Recent Trends in the Conduct of International Arbitration: Discovery Procedures and Witness Hearings", 17 J. Int'l Arb. 19 (No. 2, 2000)

HAGBERG (LENNART)

"Evidence in Swedish Arbitral Procedure", 1982 Y.B. Swed.& Int'l Arb 29.

HEUMAN L.

Current Issues in Swedish Arbitration (Deventer and Stockholm 1990)

VAN HOUTTE (HANS)

Conduct of Arbitral Proceedings, in Essays on International Commercial Arbitration 113 (P. Sarcevic ed. (1989))

HUNTER (MARTIN)

"Modern Trends in the Presentation of Evidence in International Commercial Arbitration", 3 (1992) Am Rev Int Arb 204

HILL, M. & SINICROPI, A.

Evidence in Arbitration (2nd cd., Washington, D.C. 1987)

KAZAZI (MOJTABA)

Burden of Proof and Related Issues: A Study on Evidence Before International Tribunals (1996)

KOKOTT (JULIANE)

The Burden of Proof in Comparative and International Human Rights Law: Civil and Common Law Approaches with Special Reference to the American and German Legal Systems (1998)

KRONKE (HERBERT)

"Taking of Evidence Under the UNIDROIT/American Law Institute Project 'Transnational Principles of Civil Procedure'" 1 Stockholm Arb. Rep. 63 (2000)

LÉVY (LAURENT)

"Witness Statements", in De Lege Ferenda, Studies for Professor Alain Hirsch, compiled and published by Anne Héritier Lachat and Laurent Hirsch, Slatkine Geneva 2004, pp. 95-104

MARRIOTT (ARTHUR)

"Evidence in International Arbitration" 5 Arb Int'l 280 (1989)

VON MEHREN (ROBERT B.)

Burden of Proof in International Arbitration, in ICCA, Twelfth Int'l Arb. Congress: Proceedings 123 (1994)

MELIS (WERNER)

"Presentation of Documentary Evidence and Witnesses", in ICCA, Tenth Int'l Arb. Congress: Proceedings 511 (1990)

DE MELLO (XAVIER)

"International Bar Association: Régles complémentaires de preuve a usage de l'arbitrage international: commentaire", 1986 Rev. Arb. 660

MISRA (G.M.)

"Suggestions Regarding Unification of Guidelines for Presentation of Evidence in International Arbitration", in ICCA, Fifth Int'l Arb. Congress: Proceedings C IIh 1-2 (1975)

MURPHY (EWELL E. J).

"Confronting the Confrontation of the World's Two Great Arbitration Systems", A.B.A., The Int'l Arb. Rev., Summer 2003

NARAYAN (PRAKASH) & (RAGHUBIR) MEANON

Presentation of Evidence in International Commercial Arbitration – A Comparative Study, 4 Vindobona J. Int'l Com. L. & Arb. 105 (No. 2, 200)

NARIMAN (FALI S.)

Presentation of Documentary Evidence and Witnesses: The Indian Experience, in ICCA, Tenth Int'l Arb. Congress: Proceedings 493 (1990)

NEWMAN (LAWRENCE W.)

"International Litigation. Evidence in Arbitration", The New York Law Journal, September 29, 1999

PARK (WILLIAM W.)

"Arbitration's Discontents: Of Elephants and Pornography", Mealey's International Arbitration Report February 2002 Volume 17(2) 20

PATOCCHI (PAOLO MICHELE) & MEAKIN (IAN L.)

"Procedure and the Taking of Evidence in International Commercial Arbitration: The Interaction of Civil Law and Common Law Procedures", Int'l Bus. L.J. 884 (No. 7, 1996)

PAULSSON (JAN)

"Overview of Methods of Presenting Evidence in Different Legal Systems", in ICCA, Twelth Int'l Arb. Congress: Proceedings 112 (1994)

"The Rules of Evidence in the Arbitral Procedure: Comparative Study", in Euro-Arab Arbitration II 90 (F. Kernicha ed. 1989)

PERROT (ROGER)

The Civil Law Approach to Evidence, 41 Arbitration 75 (1974)

PETER (WOLFGANG)

"Witness Conferencing", 18 Arb. Int'l 47 (2002)

RAU (ALUN SCOTT) & SHERMAN (EDWARD F.)

"Tradition and Innovation in International Arbitration Procedure", 30 Tex. Int'l L.J. 89 (1995)

REED (LUCY) AND & SUTCLIFFE (JONATHAN)

"The 'Americanization' of International Arbitration?", Mealey's Int'l Arb. Rep., No. 16-4, at 37 (Apr. 2001)

REYMOND (CLAUDE)

"Civil and Common Law Procedures: Which is the More Inquisitorial?" A Civil Lawyer's Response, (1989) 5 Arb Int 357

ROBERT (JEAN)

Administration of Evidence in International Commercial Arbitration, 1 Y.B. Com Arb. 221 (1976)

ROKISON (KENNETH S.)

"The Sources and Limits of the Arbitrator's Powers in England", in Contemporary Problems of International Arbitration 86 (J.D.M. Lew ed., 1986); also 52 Arbitration 219 (1986)

RUBINO-SAMMARTANO (MAURO)

A Civil Law Approach to the UNCITRAL Model Law and to Arbitral Rules of Evidence, 51 Arbitration 278 (1985)

"La legge uniforme arbitrale delle Nazioni Unit", in Embrione, e le rules of evidence arbitrali, 39 Foro Padano 97 (1984)

"La prova nell'arbitrato internazional. Necessità (a) di una disciplina e (b) di armonizzazione", 26 Rassegna dell'Arb. 37 (1986)

"Rules of Evidence in International Arbitration: A Need for Discipline and Harmonization", 3 J. Int'l Arb. 87 (No. 2, 1986); also in 53 Arbitration 85 (1987)

RUBINO-SAMMARTANO (MAURO)
"The Civil Law Approach to Evidence", 48 Arbitration 331 (1983)

RUHLMANN (FRANÇOIS) & GUTKES (OLIVIER)
"L'absence de régles de preuve spécifique dans les arbitrages internationaux: remédes souhaitables", Int'l Bus. L. Rev. 437 (1995)

SALEH (SAMIR A.)
"Reflections on Admissibility of Evidence: Interrelation Between Domestic Law and International Arbitration", 15 Arb. Int'l 141 (1999)

SANDIFER (DUWARD V.),
Evidence Before International Tribunals (rev. ed. 1975)

SCHNEIDER (MICHAEL E.)
Les témoins dans la procédure arbitrale – Partie II, 11 Bull. Swiss Arb. A. 568 (1993)

Witnesses in International Arbitration, 11 Bull. Swiss Arb. A. 302 (1993)

"Hearing Witnesses in International Arbitration", International Commercial Litigation, February 1996, 14

SEBESTYN (G.)
"Arbitration Procedure for Evidence", in ICCA, Fifth Int'l Arb. Congress: Proceedings C IId 1-2 (1975)

SMIT (HANS)
"Roles of the Arbitral Tribunal in Civil Law and Common Law Systems with Respect to Presentation of Evidence", in ICCA, Twelth Int'l Arb. Congress Review 7 (1994)

STAUGHTON (CHRISTOPHER)
"Common Law and Civil Law Procedures: Which is the More Inquisitorial? A Common Lawyer's Response", 5 Arb Int 351 (1989)

STRAUS (MICHAEL)
"The Practice of the Iran-US Claims Tribunal in Receiving Evidence from Parties and from Experts", 3 J. Int'l Arb. 57 (No. 3, 1986)

STRENGER (IRENEU)
"Formaçao da prova no litígio arbitral", in Arbitragem 157 (P.B. Casel la ed., 1996)

SUTTON (DAVID ST. J.)

"Discovery and Production of Evidence in Arbitral Proceedings: the US and England Distinguished", in ICC, Taking of Evidence in International Proceedings 57 (1990)

TACKABERRY (JOHN A.)

"The Conduct of Arbitration Proceedings under English Law", in Contemporary Problems in International Arbitration 216 (J.D.M. Lew ed., 1986); also 52 Arbitration 227 (1986)

THORENS (JUSTIN)

"L'arbitre international au point de rencontre des traditions du droit civil et de la common law. Deux problèmes liés l'un à la communication des piéces et l'autre à l'auditions des témoins", in Etudes de droit international en l'honneur de Pierre Lalive 693 (Ch. Dominicé & C. Reymond, eds. 1993)

TIBREWAL (S.)

"Presenting Evidence in International Commercial Arbitration", in ICCA, Fifth Int'l Arb. Congress: Proceedings C IIf 1-5 (1975)

TRIEBEL (VOLKER)

"An Outline of the Swiss/German Rules of Civil Procedure and Practice Relating to Evidence", 47 Arbitration 221 (1982)

"Rules of Procedure and Practice Relating to Evidence in Arbitration Proceedings in Continental Europe", 16 Indian Council of Arbitration Q. 3 (No. 4, Jan.-March 1982)

TUPMAN (W. MICHAEL)

Discovery and Evidence in US Arbitration: The Prevailing Views, 44 Arb. J. 27 (No. 1, 1989)

WALDER-BOHNER (HANS ULRICH),

"Zeugen vor Schiedsgericht", in Recueil de Travaux Suisses 213 (C. Reymond & F. Bucher, eds. 1984)

WARD (ROGER K)

"The Flexibility of Evidentiary Rules in International Trade Dispute Arbitration: Problems Posed to American-Trained Lawyers", 13 J. Int'l Arb. 5 (No. 3, 1996)

B. ETHICS AND ORAL EVIDENCE

Council of the Bars and Law Societies of the European Community (CCBE) Code of Conduct

Constitution of the Association of Defence Counsel for the ICTY, Archbold's International Criminal Court (2003; B4-001, p.955)

BROWER (CHARLES N.)

"Evidence Before International Tribunals: The Need for Some Standard Rules", 18 Int'l Law. 47 (1994)

DRAHOZAL (CHRISTOPHER R.)

"Commercial Norms, Commercial Codes and International Commercial Arbitration", 33 Vand. J. Transnat'l L. 79 (2000)

VAN HOUTTE, HANS

"Counsel-Witness Relations and Professional Misconduct in Civil Law Systems", (2003) 19 Arb Int. 457

IBA International Code of Legal Ethics, reprinted in "Law Without Frontiers: A Comparative Survey of the Rules of Professional Ethics Applicable to the Cross-Border Practice of Law", 361-362 (Edwin Godfrey ed., 1995)

JARVIS (ROBERT M.)

"Cross-Border Legal Practice and Ethics Rule 4-8.5: Why Greater Guidance Is Needed", 72 Fla. G.J. 59 (1998)

MCCARY (MARK)

Note, "Bridging Ethical Borders: International Legal Ethics with an Islamic Perspective", 35 Tex. Int'l L.J., 313 (2000)

MCCONNAUGHAY (PHILIP J.)

"The Risks and Virtues of Lawlessness: A 'Second Look' at International Commercial Arbitration", 93 Nw. U.L. Rev. 453 (1999)

MULLERAT (RAMON)

"Is a Global Code of Ethics Attainable", 58(2) Int Bar News 33, 2004

NEWMAN (LAWRENCE N.)

"International Litigation. Ethics in Arbitration", The New York Law Journal, July 31, 2000

PARK (WILLIAM W.)

"National Law and Commercial Justice: Safeguarding Procedural Integrity in International Arbitration", 63 Tul. L. Rev. 647 (1989)

PAULSSON (JAN)

"Ethics and Codes of Conduct for a Multi-Disciplinary Institute", Arbitration 193, 2004

"Standards of Conduct for Counsel in International Arbitration", 3 Am. Rev. Int. Arb. 214 (1992)

PIORKOWSKI (JOSEPH D. JR)

"Note, Professional Conduct and the Preparation of Witnesses for Trial: Defining the Acceptable Limitations of "Coaching", 1 Geo. J. Legal Ethics 389 (1987)

ROGERS (CATHERINE)

"Fit and Function in Legal Ethics: Developing a Code of Conduct for International Arbitration", 23 Mich, J. Int'l L. 341 (2002)

ROTH (MARIANNE)

"Consequences and Prevention of False Evidence Under the English Arbitration Act 1996: A Comparative Perspective", 13 Arb. Int'l 391 (1997)

"False Testimony at International Arbitration Hearings Conducted in England and Switzerland – A Comparative View", 11 J. Int'l Arb. 5 (No. 1, 1994)

TOULMIN (JOHN)

"A Worldwide Common Code of Professional Ethics?", 15 Fordham Int'l L.J. 673 (1992)

ULMER (NICOLAS)

"Ethics and Effectiveness: Doing Well by Doing Good", The Commercial Way to Justice: An International Arbitration Conference (1996)

VAGTS (DETLEV F.)

"The International Legal Profession: A Need for More Governance?", 90 Am. J. Intl. 250 (1996)

"Professional Responsibility in Transborder Practice: Conflict and Resolution", 13 Geo. J. Legal Ethics 677 (2000)

VEEDER (V.V.)
The 2001 Goff Lecture: The Lawyer's Duty to Arbitrate in Good Faith, (2002) 18 Arb Int 431

WETTER (J. GILLIS)
"The Case for International Law Schools and an International Legal Profession", (1980) 20 ICLQ 206

ZACHARIAS (FRED C.)
"Reconceptualizing Ethical Roles", 65 Geo. Wash. L. Rev. 169 (1997)

C. IBA RULES OF EVIDENCE

"IBA Rules on the Taking of Evidence in International Commercial Arbitration" (adopted June 1999) (1999) XXIVa ICCA Yearbook 410

BÜHLER (MICHAEL) AND DORGAN (CAROLL)
"Witness Testimony Pursuant to the 1999 IBA Rules of Evidence in International Commercial Arbitration. Novel or Tested Standards?", Journal of International Arbitration, 17(1): 3, 2000

DARWAZEH (NADIA)
"Document Discovery and the IBA Rules on Evidence: A Practitioner's View", (2002) 4 Int Arb Law Rev 101

RAESCHKE-KESSLER (HILMAR)
"The Production of Documents in International Arbitration: A Commentary on Art. 3 of the New "IBA-Rules of Evidence", in Law of International Business and Dispute Settlement in the 21st Century: Liber Amicorum Karl-Heinz Böckstiegel 641 R. Briner, L.Y. Fortier, K.P. Berger & J. Bredow, eds. (2001); also 18 Arb Int'l 411 (2002)

RIVKIN (DAVID)
"IBA Rules on the Taking of Evidence in International Commercial Arbitration", XIVA ICCA Yearbook 408 (1999)

SANDERS (PIETER)
"The Work of UNCITRAL on Arbitration and Conciliation" (2nd ed.; 2004), pp 18-22, 24-28, 30-37

SHENTON (DAVID W.)

"An Introduction to the IBA Rules of Evidence", 1 Arbitration Int'l 118 (1985); also in 51 Arbitration 553 (Nov. 1985)

"Supplementary Rules Governing the Presentation and Reception of Evidence in International Commercial Arbitration", (1985) X ICCA Yearbook. 145; also Contemporary Problems in Int'l Arbitration 188 (J.D.M. Lew ed., 1986)

VEEDER (V.V.)

"Evidential Rules in International Commercial Arbitration: From the Tower of London to the New 1999 IBA Rules", Arbitration 115 (1999)

Case Law Index

Key-words Index

With the kind help of Vincent SIEBER, Legal Intern, Schellenberg Wittmer, Switzerland

A

B

C

D

E

H

I

J

L

P

Q

R

S

T

IBA Rules on the taking of evidence in international commercial arbitration*

THE RULES

Preamble

1. These IBA Rules on the Taking of Evidence in International Commercial Arbitration (the "IBA Rules of Evidence") are intended to govern in an efficient and economical manner the taking of evidence in international commercial arbitrations, particularly those between Parties from different legal traditions. They are designed to supplement the legal provisions and the institutional or *ad hoc* rules according to which the Parties are conducting their arbitration.
2. Parties and Arbitral Tribunals may adopt the IBA Rules of Evidence, in whole or in part, to govern arbitration proceedings, or they may vary them or use them as guidelines in developing their own procedures. The Rules are not intended to limit the flexibility that is inherent in, and an advantage of, international arbitration, and Parties and Arbitral Tribunals are free to adapt them to the particular circumstances of each arbitration.
3. Each arbitral tribunal is encouraged to identify to the Parties, as soon as it considers it to be appropriate, the issues that it may regard as relevant and material to the outcome of the case, including issues where a preliminary determination may be appropriate.
4. The taking of evidence shall be conducted on the principle that each Party shall be entitled to know, reasonably in advance of any evidentiary hearing, the evidence on which the other Parties rely.

---

* Adopted by a resolution of the IBA Council, 1 June 1999.
This document is reproduced by kind permission of the International Bar Association, London.

THE RULES

Article 1 – Definitions

In the IBA Rules of Evidence:

"Arbitral tribunal" means a sole arbitrator or a panel of arbitrators validly deciding by majority or otherwise;

"Claimant" means the Party or Parties who commenced the arbitration and any Party who, through joinder or otherwise, becomes aligned with such Party or Parties;

"Document" means a writing of any kind, whether recorded on paper, electronic means, audio or visual recordings or any other mechanical or electronic means of storing or recording information;

"Evidentiary hearing" means any hearing, whether or not held on consecutive days, at which the arbitral tribunal receives oral evidence;

"Expert Report" means a written statement by a tribunal-appointed expert or a party-appointed expert submitted pursuant to the IBA Rules of Evidence;

"General Rules" mean the institutional or *ad hoc* rules according to which the Parties are conducting their arbitration;

"Party" means a party to the arbitration;

"Party-appointed expert" means an expert-witness presented by a Party;

"Request to Produce" means a request by a Party for a procedural order by which the arbitral tribunal would direct another Party to produce documents;

"Respondent" means the Party or Parties against whom the Claimant made its claim, and any Party who, through joinder or otherwise, becomes aligned with such Party or Parties, and includes a Respondent making a counter-claim;

"tribunal-appointed expert" means a person or organization appointed by the arbitral tribunal in order to report to it on specific issues determined by the arbitral tribunal.

Article 2 – Scope of application

1. Whenever the Parties have agreed or the arbitral tribunal has determined to apply the IBA Rules of Evidence, the Rules shall govern the taking of evidence, except to the extent that any specific provision of them may be found to be in conflict with any mandatory provision of law determined to be applicable to the case by the Parties or by the arbitral tribunal.
2. In case of conflict between any provisions of the IBA Rules of Evidence and the General Rules, the arbitral tribunal shall apply the IBA Rules of Evidence in the manner that it determines best in order to accomplish the purposes of both the General Rules and the IBA Rules of Evidence, unless the Parties agree to the contrary.
3. In the event of any dispute regarding the meaning of the IBA Rules of Evidence, the arbitral tribunal shall interpret them according to their purpose and in the manner most appropriate for the particular arbitration.
4. Insofar as the IBA Rules of Evidence and the General Rules are silent on any matter concerning the taking of evidence and the Parties have not agreed otherwise, the arbitral tribunal may conduct the taking of evidence as it deems appropriate, in accordance with the general principles of the IBA Rules of Evidence.

Article 3 – Documents

1. Within the time ordered by the arbitral tribunal, each Party shall submit to the arbitral tribunal and to the other Parties all documents available to it on which it relies, including public documents and those in the public domain, except for any documents that have already been submitted by another Party.
2. Within the time ordered by the arbitral tribunal, any Party may submit to the arbitral tribunal a Request to Produce.
3. A Request to Produce shall contain:
   a) (i) a description of a requested document sufficient to identify it, or
   (ii) a description in sufficient detail (including subject matter) of a narrow and specific requested category of documents that are reasonably believed to exist;

b) a description of how the documents requested are relevant and material to the outcome of the case; and
c) a statement that the documents requested are not in the possession, custody or control of the requesting Party, and of the reason why that Party assumes the documents requested to be in the possession, custody or control of the other Party.

4. Within the time ordered by the arbitral tribunal, the Party to whom the Request to Produce is addressed shall produce to the arbitral tribunal and to the other Parties all the documents requested in its possession, custody or control as to which no objection is made.

5. If the Party to whom the Request to Produce is addressed has objections to some or all of the documents requested, it shall state them in writing to the arbitral tribunal within the time ordered by the arbitral tribunal. The reasons for such objections shall be any of those set forth in Article 9.2.

6. The arbitral tribunal shall, in consultation with the Parties and in timely fashion, consider the Request to Produce and the objections. The arbitral tribunal may order the Party to whom such Request is addressed to produce to the arbitral tribunal and to the other Parties those requested documents in its possession, custody or control as to which the arbitral tribunal determines that (i) the issues that the requesting Party wishes to prove are relevant and material to the outcome of the case, and (ii) none of the reasons for objection set forth in Article 9.2 apply.

7. In exceptional circumstances, if the propriety of an objection can only be determined by review of the document, the arbitral tribunal may determine that it should not review the document. In that event, the arbitral tribunal may, after consultation with the Parties, appoint an independent and impartial expert, bound to confidentiality, to review any such document and to report on the objection. To the extent that the objection is upheld by the arbitral tribunal, the expert shall not disclose to the arbitral tribunal and to the other Parties the contents of the document reviewed.

8. If a Party wishes to obtain the production of documents from a person or organization who is not a Party to the arbitration and from whom the Party cannot obtain the documents on its own, the Party may, within the time ordered by the arbitral tribunal, ask it to take whatever steps are legally available to obtain the requested documents. The Party shall identify the

documents in sufficient detail and state why such documents are relevant and material to the outcome of the case. The arbitral tribunal shall decide on this request and shall take the necessary steps if in its discretion it determines that the documents would be relevant and material.

9. The arbitral tribunal, at any time before the arbitration is concluded, may request a Party to produce to the arbitral tribunal and to the other Parties any documents that it believes to be relevant and material to the outcome of the case. A Party may object to such a request based on any of the reasons set forth in Article 9.2. If a Party raises such an objection, the arbitral tribunal shall decide whether to order the production of such documents based upon the considerations set forth in Article 3.6 and, if the arbitral tribunal considers it appropriate, through the use of the procedures set forth in Article 3.7.

10. Within the time ordered by the arbitral tribunal, the Parties may submit to the arbitral tribunal and to the other Parties any additional documents which they believe have become relevant and material as a consequence of the issues raised in documents, Witness Statements or Expert Reports submitted or produced by another Party or in other submissions of the Parties.

11. If copies are submitted or produced, they must conform fully to the originals. At the request of the arbitral tribunal, any original must be presented for inspection.

12. All documents produced by a Party pursuant to the IBA Rules of Evidence (or by a non-Party pursuant to Article 3.8) shall be kept confidential by the arbitral tribunal and by the other Parties, and they shall be used only in connection with the arbitration. The arbitral tribunal may issue orders to set forth the terms of this confidentiality. This requirement is without prejudice to all other obligations of confidentiality in arbitration.

Article 4 – Witnesses of fact

1. Within the time ordered by the arbitral tribunal, each Party shall identify the witnesses on whose testimony it relies and the subject matter of that testimony.

2. Any person may present evidence as a witness, including a Party or a Party's officer, employee or other representative.

3. It shall not be improper for a Party, its officers, employees, legal advisors or other representatives to interview its witnesses or potential witnesses.

4. The arbitral tribunal may order each Party to submit within a specified time to the arbitral tribunal and to the other Parties a written statement by each witness on whose testimony it relies, except for those witnesses whose testimony is sought pursuant to Article 4.10 (the "Witness Statement"). If evidentiary hearings are organized on separate issues (such as liability and damages), the arbitral tribunal or the Parties by agreement may schedule the submission of Witness Statements separately for each evidentiary hearing.

5. Each Witness Statement shall contain:
   a) the full name and address of the witness, his or her present and past relationship (if any) with any of the Parties, and a description of his or her background, qualifications, training and experience, if such a description may be relevant and material to the dispute or to the contents of the statement;
   b) a full and detailed description of the facts, and the source of the witness's information as to those facts, sufficient to serve as that witness's evidence in the matter in dispute;
   c) an affirmation of the truth of the statement; and
   d) the signature of the witness and its date and place.

6. If Witness Statements are submitted, any Party may, within the time ordered by the arbitral tribunal, submit to the arbitral tribunal and to the other Parties revised or additional Witness Statements, including statements from persons not previously named as witnesses, so long as any such revisions or additions only respond to matters contained in another Party's Witness Statement or Expert Report and such matters have not been previously presented in the arbitration.

7. Each witness who has submitted a Witness Statement shall appear for testimony at an evidentiary hearing, unless the Parties agree otherwise.

8. If a witness who has submitted a Witness Statement does not appear without a valid reason for testimony at an evidentiary hearing, except by agreement of the Parties, the arbitral tribunal shall disregard that Witness Statement unless, in exceptional circumstances, the arbitral tribunal determines otherwise.

9. If the Parties agree that a witness who has submitted a Witness Statement does not need to appear for testimony at an evidentiary hearing, such an agreement shall not be considered to reflect an agreement as to the correctness of the content of the Witness Statement.

10. If a Party wishes to present evidence from a person who will not appear voluntarily at its request, the Party may, within the time ordered by the arbitral tribunal, ask it to take whatever steps are legally available to obtain the testimony of that person. The Party shall identify the intended witness, shall describe the subjects on which the witness's testimony is sought and shall state why such subjects are relevant and material to the outcome of the case. The arbitral tribunal shall decide on this request and shall take the necessary steps if in its discretion it determines that the testimony of that witness would be relevant and material.

11. The arbitral tribunal may, at any time before the arbitration is concluded, order any Party to provide, or to use its best efforts to provide, the appearance for testimony at an evidentiary hearing of any person, including one whose testimony has not yet been offered.

Article 5 – Party-appointed experts

1. A Party may rely on a party-appointed expert as a means of evidence on specific issues. Within the time ordered by the arbitral tribunal, a party-appointed expert shall submit an Expert Report.

2. The Expert Report shall contain:
   a) the full name and address of the party-appointed expert, his or her present and past relationship (if any) with any of the Parties, and a description of his or her background, qualifications, training and experience;
   b) a statement of the facts on which he or she is basing his or her expert opinions and conclusions;
   c) his or her expert opinions and conclusions, including a description of the method, evidence and information used in arriving at the conclusions;
   d) an affirmation of the truth of the Expert Report; and
   e) the signature of the party-appointed expert and its date and place.

3. The arbitral tribunal in its discretion may order that any party-appointed experts who have submitted Expert Reports on the same or related issues meet and confer on such issues. At such meeting, the party-appointed experts shall attempt to reach agreement on those issues as to which they had differences of opinion in their Expert Reports, and they shall record in writing any such issues on which they reach agreement.
4. Each party-appointed expert shall appear for testimony at an evidentiary hearing, unless the Parties agree otherwise and the arbitral tribunal accepts this agreement.
5. If a party-appointed expert does not appear without a valid reason for testimony at an evidentiary hearing, except by agreement of the Parties accepted by the arbitral tribunal, the arbitral tribunal shall disregard his or her Expert Report unless, in exceptional circumstances, the arbitral tribunal determines otherwise.
6. If the Parties agree that a party-appointed expert does not need to appear for testimony at an evidentiary hearing, such an agreement shall not be considered to reflect an agreement as to the correctness of the content of the Expert Report.

Article 6 – Tribunal-appointed experts

1. The arbitral tribunal, after having consulted with the Parties, may appoint one or more independent tribunal-appointed experts to report to it on specific issues designated by the arbitral tribunal. The arbitral tribunal shall establish the terms of reference for any tribunal-appointed expert report after having consulted with the Parties. A copy of the final terms of reference shall be sent by the arbitral tribunal to the Parties.
2. The tribunal-appointed expert shall, before accepting appointment, submit to the arbitral tribunal and to the Parties a statement of his or her independence from the Parties and the arbitral tribunal. Within the time ordered by the arbitral tribunal, the Parties shall inform the arbitral tribunal whether they have any objections to the tribunal-appointed expert's independence. The arbitral tribunal shall decide promptly whether to accept any such objection.

3. Subject to the provisions of Article 9.2, the Tribunal-Appointed Expert may request a Party to provide any relevant and material information or to provide access to any relevant documents, goods, samples, property or site for inspection.

4. The authority of a tribunal-appointed expert to request such information or access shall be the same as the authority of the arbitral tribunal. The Parties and their representatives shall have the right to receive any such information and to attend any such inspection. Any disagreement between a tribunal-appointed expert and a Party as to the relevance, materiality or appropriateness of such a request shall be decided by the arbitral tribunal, in the manner provided in Articles 3.5 through 3.7. The tribunal-appointed expert shall record in the report any non-compliance by a Party with an appropriate request or decision by the arbitral tribunal and shall describe its effects on the determination of the specific issue.

5. The tribunal-appointed expert shall report in writing to the arbitral tribunal. The tribunal-appointed expert shall describe in the report the method, evidence and information used in arriving at the conclusions.

6. The arbitral tribunal shall send a copy of such Expert Report to the Parties. The Parties may examine any document that the tribunal-appointed expert has examined and any correspondence between the arbitral tribunal and the tribunal-appointed expert. Within the time ordered by the arbitral tribunal, any Party shall have the opportunity to respond to the report in a submission by the Party or through an Expert Report by a party-appointed expert. The arbitral tribunal shall send the submission or Expert Report to the tribunal-appointed expert and to the other Parties.

7. At the request of a Party or of the arbitral tribunal, the Tribunal-Appointed Expert shall be present at an evidentiary hearing. The arbitral tribunal may question the tribunal-appointed expert, and he or she may be questioned by the Parties or by any party-appointed expert on issues raised in the Parties' submissions or in the Expert Reports made by the party-appointed experts pursuant to Article 6.5.

8. Any Expert Report made by a tribunal-appointed expert and its conclusions shall be assessed by the arbitral tribunal with due regard to all circumstances of the case.

9. The fees and expenses of a tribunal-appointed expert, to be funded in a manner determined by the arbitral tribunal, shall form part of the costs of the arbitration.

Article 7 – On site inspection

Subject to the provisions of Article 9.2, the arbitral tribunal may, at the request of a Party or on its own motion, inspect or require the inspection by a tribunal-appointed expert of any site, property, machinery or any other goods or process, or documents, as it deems appropriate. The arbitral tribunal shall, in consultation with the Parties, determine the timing and arrangement for the inspection. The Parties and their representatives shall have the right to attend any such inspection.

Article 8 – Evidentiary hearing

1. The arbitral tribunal shall at all times have complete control over the evidentiary hearing. The arbitral tribunal may limit or exclude any question to, answer by or appearance of a witness (which term includes, for the purposes of this Article, witnesses of fact and any Experts), if it considers such question, answer or appearance to be irrelevant, immaterial, burdensome, duplicative or covered by a reason for objection set forth in Article 9.2. Questions to a witness during direct and redirect testimony may not be unreasonably leading.

2. The Claimant shall ordinarily first present the testimony of its witnesses, followed by the Respondent presenting testimony of its witnesses, and then by the presentation by Claimant of rebuttal witnesses, if any. Following direct testimony, any other Party may question such witness, in an order to be determined by the arbitral tribunal. The Party who initially presented the witness shall subsequently have the opportunity to ask additional questions on the matters raised in the other Parties' questioning. The arbitral tribunal, upon request of a Party or on its own motion, may vary this order of proceeding, including the arrangement of testimony by particular issues or in such a manner that witnesses presented by different Parties be questioned at the same time and in confrontation with each other. The arbitral tribunal may ask questions to a witness at any time.

3. Any witness providing testimony shall first affirm, in a manner determined appropriate by the arbitral tribunal, that he or she is telling the truth. If the witness has submitted a Witness Statement or an Expert Report, the witness shall confirm it. The Parties may agree or the arbitral tribunal may order that the Witness Statement or Expert Report shall serve as that witness's direct testimony.

4. Subject to the provisions of Article 9.2, the arbitral tribunal may request any person to give oral or written evidence on any issue that the arbitral tribunal considers to be relevant and material. Any witness called and questioned by the arbitral tribunal may also be questioned by the Parties.

Article 9 – Admissibility and assessment of evidence

1. The arbitral tribunal shall determine the admissibility, relevance, materiality and weight of evidence.

2. The arbitral tribunal shall, at the request of a Party or on its own motion, exclude from evidence or production any document, statement, oral testimony or inspection for any of the following reasons:
   a) lack of sufficient relevance or materiality;
   b) legal impediment or privilege under the legal or ethical rules determined by the arbitral tribunal to be applicable;
   c) unreasonable burden to produce the requested evidence;
   d) loss or destruction of the document that has been reasonably shown to have occurred;
   e) grounds of commercial or technical confidentiality that the arbitral tribunal determines to be compelling;
   f) grounds of special political or institutional sensitivity (including evidence that has been classified as secret by a government or a public international institution) that the arbitral tribunal determines to be compelling; or
   g) considerations of fairness or equality of the Parties that the arbitral tribunal determines to be compelling.

3. The arbitral tribunal may, where appropriate, make necessary arrangements to permit evidence to be considered subject to suitable confidentiality protection.

If a Party fails without satisfactory explanation to produce any document requested in a Request to Produce to which it has not objected in due time or fails to produce any document ordered to be produced by the arbitral tribunal, the arbitral tribunal may infer that such document would be adverse to the interests of that Party.

4. If a Party fails without satisfactory explanation to make available any other relevant evidence, including testimony, sought by one Party to which the Party to whom the request was addressed has not objected in due time or fails to make available any evidence, including testimony, ordered by the arbitral tribunal to be produced, the arbitral tribunal may infer that such evidence would be adverse to the interests of that Party.

Contributors

DAVID BROWN

is the Managing Partner of the Paris office of Shadbolt & Co, and practices as both an English solicitor and an avocat at the Paris Bar, specialising in international arbitration both as counsel and arbitrator. He and his firm are particularly involved in construction-related work, and he also has a wide-ranging practice in international trade and joint venturing arrangements. He is a Council Member of the ICC Institute.

ANTONIAS DIMOLITSA

is a Partner of the law firm A. Dimolitsa & Associates, Greece. She is a Council Member of the ICC Institute, former Member of the International Court of Arbitration and Vice-President of the Forum ICC Rules/Court in the ICC Commission on International Arbitration. She is also Member of the Council of the Greek Arbitration Association.

PAUL-A. GÉLINAS

is Member of the Montreal and Paris Bars. He is the former Chairman of the ICC Commission on International Arbitration (1994-2001) and a former Member of the International Court of Arbitration (1974-1990). He acts mainly as arbitrator and mediator. He is a Council Member of the ICC Institute.

HANS VAN HOUTTE

teaches conflicts of laws, arbitration and international business law at Leuven University -Belgium. He has served as arbitrator in well over 100 arbitrations. He has been member of the Commission for Real Property Claims in Bosnia and Herzegovina (1996-2003) and the United Nations Compensation Commission (1998-2001) as well as an Arbitrator and Senior Judge at the Claims Resolution Tribunal for Dormant Accounts in Switzerland (1999-2002). He is currently President of the Eritrea-Ethiopia Claims Commission. He is also the author of over 100 articles on arbitration and international business transactions.

RICHARD H. KREINDLER

is a Partner of the law firm Shearman & Sterling, resident in its Frankfurt office, and specialising in international arbitration and litigation matters. He is a Council Member of the ICC Institute and a Member of the ICC Commission on International Arbitration. Admitted to practice in New York and Paris, and graduated from Harvard, Munich and Columbia Universities, he is an Adjunct Professor of Law at the University of Münster (Germany) in the areas of transnational litigation and arbitration.

Serge Lazareff

is Member of the Paris Bar. He is Doctor of Law of the University of Paris and holds an LL.M. from Harvard. He is Chairman of the ICC Institute and Chairman of the French Arbitration Commission of ICC France. He was formerly General Counsel for International Operations and Vice-President Asia-pacific of Pechiney, one of the leading French industrial groups.

Laurent Lévy

Docteur en droit (University of Paris/Panthéon/Sorbonne), he is a partner of the Firm Schellenberg Wittmer (formerly Brunschwig, Biaggi, Lévy, then Brunschwig Wittmer) since 1981, specialising in international commercial arbitration, serving very often as arbitrator and also acting as counsel. His other fields of expertise are international law and commercial law. He is the author of several articles on arbitration, relating in particular to banking law, corporate law and insolvency law. He is also a Council Member of the ICC Institute.

Robert S. Rifkind

is a Senior Counsel in the New York office of the law firm Cravath, Swaine & Moore LLP, specialising in civil litigation and international arbitration. From 1965 to 1968 he served as Assistant to the Solicitor General in the United States Department of Justice in Washington, D.C. He is graduated from Yale University and Harvard Law School.

Anne Véronique Schlaepfer

is a partner of the Firm Schellenberg Wittmer since January 1, 2002, specialising in international commercial arbitration. She acts mostly as counsel in arbitration proceedings relating *inter alia* to corporate affairs, energy, joint ventures, sales.

V. V. Veeder

is Arbitrator and Advocate of Essex Court Chambers (London). He is also General Editor of "Arbitration International", Chairman of ARIAS-AIDA (UK), Council Member of the ICC Institute and Chairman IFSL Arbitration Committee.

List of attendees

Tito Arantes Fontes (Portugal), Domitille Baizeau (France), John Beechey (United Kingdom), Denis Bensaude (France), Andrew W.A. Berkeley (United Kingdom), Thibault Beurnier (France), Karl-Heinz Böckstiegel (Germany), Bruno Boesch (United Kingdom), Stephen R. Bond (France), Thierry Bonnet (France), Fabio Bortolotti (Italy), David Branson (United States), Robert Briner (France), Claes Broman (Sweden), Peter Callens (Belgium), Denny Vinston Caouki (Turkey), Emmanuel de Cannard d'Hamale (Belgium), Jurgen De Korte (Netherlands), Laetitia de Montalivet (France), Elisabeth de Nadal Clanchet (Spain), Yves Derains (France), Ugur Dogan (Turkey), Nicole Dolens-Extrale (Austria), Ahmed S. El-Kosheri (Egypt), Ercüment Erdem (Turkey), Joost Everaert (Belgium), Julietta Feliciani (France), Jean-Pierre Fierens (Belgium), Jeroen Fleming (Netherlands), Andrew Flower (France), Andre Friedman (Hungary), Alfred Gerber (Switzerland), Andrea Giardina (Italy), Peter Graham (Turkey), Jacob Grierson (France), Raouf Guiga (France), Pierre Heitzmann (France), Alain Hirsch (Switzerland), Lothar Hofmann (Austria), Pascal Hollander (Belgium), Robert Hunter (Germany), Christophe Imhoos (Switzerland), Khaled Jedidi (Tunisia), Ousmane Kane (Switzerland), Kristine Karsten (France), Isabel King-Cabot (France), Christian Konrad (Austria), Pierre Lalive (Switzerland), Giovanni Leo (Italy), Tim Maddock (Netherlands), Giorgio Massarotto (Italy), Hakan Matz (Sweden), Richard Meese (France), Mustafa K. Mennan (Turkey), Andrea Molino (Switzerland), Luis Montes Reig (Spain), Alexis Mourre (France), Alexandra Munoz (France), Nathan D. O'Malley (Netherlands), Aiman Odeh (Jordan), Attila Ozer (Turkey), Mirèze Philippe (France), Michael Polkinghorne (France), Sorin Popescu (Romania), Bruno Quint (France), Inigo Quintana Aguirre (Spain), Dietrich Raepple (Germany), José Rosell (France), Jean Rouche (France), Christian Rumpf (Germany), Antonio Sampaio Caramelo (Portugal), Joao Santos (Portugal), Gilles Sauvage (France), Mika Savola (Finland), Eric A. Schwartz (France), Franz Schwarz (United Kingdom), Estuardo Sierra (United States), Michelle Sindler (Switzerland), Maria Skagou (Greece), Geoffrey Smith (France), Hansjörg Stutzer (Switzerland), Jean Timsit (France), Lourdes Tincopa (United States), Jean-François Tossens (Belgium), Annie Toubiana (France), Willem H. Van Baren (Netherlands), Vera van Houtte (Belgium), Carlos Veiga (Cape Verde), Georg H. von Segesser (Switzerland), Evangelia Vouza (Greece), Zhu Jianlin (China), Roland Ziade (France)

ICC at a glance

ICC is the world business organization, the only representative body that speaks with authority on behalf of enterprises from all sectors in every part of the world.

ICC promotes an open international trade and investment system and the market economy. Its conviction that trade is a powerful force for peace and prosperity dates from the organization's origins early in the last century. The small group of far-sighted business leaders who founded ICC called themselves "the merchants of peace".

Because its member companies and associations are themselves engaged in international business, ICC has unrivalled authority in making rules that govern the conduct of business across borders. Although these rules are voluntary, they are observed in countless thousands of transactions every day and have become part of the fabric of international trade.

ICC also provides essential services, foremost among them the ICC International Court of Arbitration, the world's leading arbitral institution.

Within a year of the creation of the United Nations, ICC was granted consultative status at the highest level with the UN and its specialized agencies.

Business leaders and experts drawn from the ICC membership establish the business stance on broad issues of trade and investment policy as well as on vital technical and sectoral subjects. These include financial services, information technologies, telecommunications, marketing ethics, the environment, transportation, competition law and intellectual property, among others.

ICC was founded in 1919. Today it groups thousands of member companies and associations from over 130 countries. National committees work with their members to address the concerns of business in their countries and convey to their governments the business views formulated by ICC.

Some ICC Services:

- ICC International Court of Arbitration (Paris)
- ICC International Centre for Expertise (Paris)
- ICC World Chambers Federation (Paris)
- ICC Institute of World Business Law (Paris)
- ICC Centre for Maritime Co-operation (London)
- ICC Commercial Crime Services (London), grouping:
  - The ICC Counterfeiting Intelligence Bureau
  - The ICC Commercial Crime Bureau
  - The ICC International Maritime Bureau

ICC Publishing S.A.

ICC Publishing, the publishing arm of ICC, produces and sells the works of ICC commissions and experts as well as guides and corporate handbooks on a range of business topics. Some 100 titles – designed for anyone interested in international trade – are available from ICC Publishing.

For more detailed information on ICC publications and on the above-listed activities, and to receive the programme of ICC events, please contact ICC Headquarters in Paris or the ICC national committee in your country.

Selected ICC publications

E: English – F: French – D: German – S: Spanish – I: Italian – EF: bilingual

INTERNATIONAL ARBITRATION

Arbitration - Money Laundering, Corruption and Fraud

By the ICC Institute of World Business Law

This book, containing the proceedings of a conference on arbitration and money laundering organized by the ICC Institute of World Business Law, focuses on both the nature of the problem and the response to it in legal and arbitration circles. Is the arbitrator's role in a case of fraud different from that in other disputes? Is the arbitrator bound to report a case of money laundering or fraud if he has a suspicion that something is wrong? Do counsel have an obligation to report someone who approaches them for advice on these matters? These are just some of the key issues considered in this timely publication.

E 192 pages ISBN 92-842-1320-7 No. 651

Complex Arbitrations

Business transactions today are rarely simple. Consequently, when disputes arise, they can be highly complex and far-reaching. This book examines the particular challenges such disputes raise for international arbitration, which, unlike litigation, relies fundamentally on the principle of party autonomy. *Complex Arbitrations* comprises a collection of articles by renowned arbitration specialists. They each deal with a specific procedural issue arising from cases involving multiple parties or contracts, or concerning matters already determined or ongoing. The anthology includes an account of the practice of the ICC International Court of Arbitration when applying the ICC Rules of Arbitration in multiparty and multi-contract cases.

E 88 pages ISBN 92-842-1331-2 No. 688

Collection of ICC Arbitral Awards, Vol. IV (1996-2000)

By Jean-Jacques Arnaldez, Yves Derains, Dominique Hascher

The latest *Collection of ICC Arbitral Awards* contains extracts of cases handled by the ICC Court of Arbitration, with indexes from preceding volumes dating back to 1974. It contains a consolidated analytical table with extensive cross-references based on the terminology used in awards and case notes; a chronological index listing the awards and containing references to legal literature; a key word index; and a cross-referenced index of cases referring to the *Journal du droit international*, the *Yearbook Commercial Arbitration* and the *International Construction Law Review* for each of the awards published in the Collection. Co-published with Kluwer International.

EF 850 pages ISBN 92-842-0316-3 No. 647

ICC Arbitration, 3rd edition

By Craig, Park and Paulsson

A hands-on guide covering every aspect of ICC arbitration, the most prevalent form of institutional arbitration in the world. This valuable third edition maintains the practical approach and the lucid style of earlier editions and offers full revisions taking account of the 1998 ICC Rules of Arbitration; fully updated statistics including the period up to January 2000; and a discussion of the much-awaited judgement of the English Court of Appeal in AT&T v. Saudi Cable Co., dealing with ICC arbitrators' duties of disclosure, impartiality and independence. Published by Oceana Publications, Inc., and distributed by ICC Publishing.

E 952 pages ISBN 92-842-1251-0 No. 594

ICC International Court of Arbitration Bulletin

The *ICC International Court of Arbitration Bulletin* contains information and comment of practical relevance to businesses and their lawyers contemplating or already involved in ICC arbitration proceedings, plus the 2002 statistical report on ICC dispute resolution services.

Available by subscription. For further information, visit www.iccbooks.com.

E-F 88 pages

ANTI-CORRUPTION AND FRAUD

Corporate Governance Worldwide

A guide to best practices for managers

Today, good corporate governance – the rules and practices that govern the relationship between the managers and shareholders of corporations, as well as stakeholders (employees, pensioners and local communities) – has become a must in the modern business environment. *Corporate Governance Worldwide* provides an update of breaking developments in the field and recommendations on how business should react to new governance requirements generated by governments and the marketplace.

E 184 pages ISBN 92-842-1333-9 No. 654

Fighting Corruption – a corporate practices manual

How does a company develop a clear and enforceable code of conduct? What steps should it take to ensure that it is hiring qualified and reputable agents? How does one develop an accounting policy with explicit prohibitions against off-the-book or false entries? How does a company assess its vulnerability to money laundering and develop a know-your-customer policy? *Fighting Corruption* details concrete steps companies can take to protect themselves against unethical and unlawful acts by employees, external auditors and corporate officials.

E 244 pages ISBN 92-842-1321-5 No. 652

Preventing Financial Instrument Fraud

This invaluable reference manual and training aid by ICC Commercial Crime Services features a number of case studies that illustrate how criminals use documents to perpetrate a wide variety of very plausible scams, and how seriously the judiciary worldwide now treats this issue.

E 128 pages ISBN 92-842-1217-7 No. 648

Trade Finance Fraud

Including case studies of some of the spectacular frauds that have resulted in recent dealings, this thorough and lucid text highlights the dangers and shows how traders and financiers can protect themselves, including an in-depth study of legal recourse.

E 84 pages ISBN 92-842-1213-6 No. 643

INTERNATIONAL TRADE

Key Words in International Trade *Electronic*

Over 3000 translations of the terms and abbreviations most commonly used in international law and commerce. Now, the electronic application *Key Words in International Trade Interactive* makes access to thousands of trade terms and abbreviations even easier and more convenient – select any term instantly in any language, choose your own default search language and screen language, or access the Web sites of several organizations directly. *Key Words Interactive* is conveniently stored on your desktop or laptop hard disk for consultation both in and out of the office.

EFSDI ISBN 92-842-1187-5 No. 417/4

A to Z of International Trade

By Frank Reynolds

More than a dictionary, *A to Z* doubles as a reference book, developing terms in context and showing how they interact. Contents include over 2000 definitions and acronyms, as well as nine "Focus on" sections on air transport, bank collections, e-commerce, Incoterms, insurance, letters of credit, sales contracts, liner vessel shipping and vessel chartering.

E 343 pages ISBN 92-842-1277-4 No. 623

Guide to Export-Import Basics, 2nd edition

A fully revised edition of this ICC bestseller. Providing clear explanations of the core mechanics of trade, this guide takes a lucid look at the legal, financial, transport and e-commerce issues. Fully indexed, it also includes a handy glossary of the principal terms and abbreviations.

E 360 pages ISBN 92-842-1309-6 No. 641

www.ingramcontent.com/pod-product-compliance
Lightning Source LLC
LaVergne TN
LVHW011132300926
849160LV00008B/618